Praise for Marketing for Entrepreneurs

'Reading this book will seriously enhance your competitive advantage and your opportunities of profitable growth.'

ERIC PEACOCK, CHAIR, ACADEMY FOR CHIEF EXECUTIVES

'Whether an actor, a CEO or the owner of a small business, you have to market yourself. Jurgen Wolff reveals innovative and practical techniques that will make you a star in the marketplace.'

MICHAEL BRANDON, STAR OF *DEMPSEY AND MAKEPEACE* AND *JERRY SPRINGER: THE OPERA*

'Marketing for Entrepreneurs *is spot-on! It is a modern, bang up-to-date book for anyone who runs their own business. Written in an easy-to-read style, this book contains small-business-friendly references, case studies and examples to bring the text to life. Excellent as a marketing refresher or for the first-time marketing virgin. Buy it before your competition does!'*

ROBERT CRAVEN, KEYNOTE SPEAKER AND AUTHOR OF BUSINESS BESTSELLER, *BRIGHT MARKETING*

D0028154

Marketing

For Entrepreneurs

Jurgen Wolff

It's no longer enough to provide an outstanding product or service – the way you market your product or service must be just as outstanding, if not more.

Marketing for Entrepreneurs shows you step by step how to master the marketing of your business. You'll find out how to:

○ Get inside the mind of your customer to understand their shifting needs and respond to them quickly

○ Use branding to define the identity of your business or product and make it stick

○ Make the most of the opportunities offered by both old and new media to really get noticed

You'll gain an extensive marketing toolkit giving you scope to create and action marketing plans that will wow your customers and leave your competitors trailing behind.

For Entrepreneurs

Marketing

For Entrepreneurs

Books that make you better

Books that make you better. That make you *be* better,
do better, *feel* better. Whether you want to upgrade your
personal skills or change your job, whether you want to improve
your managerial style, become a more powerful communicator,
or be stimulated and inspired as you work.

Prentice Hall Business is leading the field with a new breed of
skills, careers and development books. Books that are a cut
above the mainstream – in topic, content and delivery – with an
edge and verve that will make you better, with less effort.

Books that are as sharp and smart as you are.

Prentice Hall Business.
We work harder – so you don't have to.

For more details on products, and to contact us, visit
www.pearsoned.co.uk

Marketing

For Entrepreneurs

Jurgen Wolff

PEARSON
Prentice Hall
BUSINESS

Harlow, England • London • New York • Boston • San Francisco • Toronto • Sydney • Singapore • Hong Kong
Tokyo • Seoul • Taipei • New Delhi • Cape Town • Madrid • Mexico City • Amsterdam • Munich • Paris • Milan

PEARSON EDUCATION LIMITED

Edinburgh Gate
Harlow CM20 2JE
Tel: +44 (0)1279 623623
Fax: +44 (0)1279 431059
Website: www.pearsoned.co.uk

First published in Great Britain in 2009

ISBN: 978-0-273-72091-1

British Library Cataloguing-in-Publication Data
A catalogue record for this book is available from the British Library

Library of Congress Cataloging-in-Publication Data
Wolff, Jurgen.
 Marketing for entrepreneurs / Jurgen Wolff.
   p. cm.
 Includes index.
 ISBN 978-0-273-72091-1 (pbk.)
 1. Marketing--Management. 2. Small business marketing. I. Title.
 HF5415.13.W653 2009
 658.8--dc22
                          2009018039

The publisher would like to thank Amanda Barry-Hirst for permission to reproduce the Prologic press release on page 73.

10 9 8 7 6 5 4 3 2 1
13 12 11 10 09

Series text design by Design Deluxe
All cartoons © Jurgen Wolff
Typeset in 9/13pt, Swis721 Lt BT by 30
Printed and bound in Great Britain by Ashford Colour Press, Gosport

The publisher's policy is to use paper manufactured from sustainable forests.

Contents

...for Entrepreneurs

Being an entrepreneur can be the path to controlling your own life and to financial success. With the *For Entrepreneurs* series, it doesn't have to be a lonely journey any more. Our expert authors guide you through all phases of starting and running a business, with practical advice every step of the way. Whether you are just getting started or want to grow your business, whether you want to become a skilled marketer or salesperson or just want to get your business finances under control, there is a *For Entrepreneurs* book ready to be your experienced, friendly and supportive business coach. Our titles include:

→ *How to Start Your Own Business for Entrepreneurs*

→ *How to Grow Your Business for Entrepreneurs*

→ *Selling for Entrepreneurs*

→ *Marketing for Entrepreneurs*

→ *Book-keeping and Accounts for Entrepreneurs*

You'll find more information and more support on our website: **www.forentrepreneursbooks.com**.

Jurgen Wolff, General Editor

About the author

Jurgen Wolff is a creativity, productivity and marketing expert whose books include *Focus: The Power of Targeted Thinking*, published by Pearson Education, and *Do Something Different*, featuring 100 case histories of creative marketing, published by Virgin Business Books.

Jurgen teaches workshops for the Academy for Chief Executives, the Cinema Extreme programme, B3 Media and many others in the UK, Europe and the United States.

His website is **www.JurgenWolff.com** and he offers a free monthly creativity and productivity e-bulletin, *Brainstorm*, which is available by email request to **BstormUK@aol.com**. He divides his time between London and the United States.

Introduction

If you have a great service or business but nobody knows about it, does it really exist? Well, probably not for long.

Yes, there are exciting new ways to get the word out, including all kinds of internet strategy, but that's not enough. As a consumer, you know how many messages you're getting sent your way every day, and the noise level is only getting higher. So how do you cut through it? That's what you'll discover in this book.

As you will see, it's simple – but not always easy. You need a guide to help you through the process, and that's what you're holding in your hands. By the time you've finished reading this book, you'll have identified your business's unique selling proposition, how to turn that into a brand, how to find the people who want and need what you're offering, how to reach them and how to persuade them. You'll have a one-year marketing plan, written in plain language, and you'll know how to turn that into daily actions.

This book is written for the businessperson who wants to find out how to stand out in today's crowded marketplace. If that's you, read on.

Your marketing mindset

Part One

Are you ready for the marketing challenge?

Chapter One

My promise: no mumbo-jumbo

There is a lot of mumbo-jumbo written about marketing, especially by professors at universities that charge an arm and a leg for their graduate business school degrees. Interestingly, many of the most successful entrepreneurs never went to a business school. In fact, many of them never attended university. Getting a degree can be beneficial in many ways (I have a couple myself), but here's a simple formula for success in business that nobody needs a degree to understand:

Step one: identify a need and create an outstanding product or service that fulfils it.

Step two: identify and locate the people most likely to benefit from your product or service and who can afford it.

Step three: convince those people of the superior benefits of your product or service.

If you do these three steps well you will succeed. Do them in a mediocre way and you'll limp along. Do them badly and you'll fail.

This book is about steps two and three. It will show you how to use the power of marketing not only to survive, but also to thrive.

As an entrepreneur you are already well aware of the challenges of doing business today. While the business world offers greater opportunities than ever before, it also presents more pitfalls – and only those who are skilled at marketing their products and services are likely to emerge triumphant.

Failure is common – but is avoidable

A few statistics are enough to tell the tale of those who fell by the wayside: a 2007 survey revealed an 11 per cent annual failure rate in the manufacturing sector and a 9 per cent failure rate in retail. Percentages don't carry a lot of emotion, so maybe a more vivid number is the 4,798 UK businesses that failed during just the first quarter of 2008 – up 8.5 per cent from the previous year – according to Experian data. Each of those nearly 5,000 failures destroyed the dreams and livelihoods of a lot of people. Since then we've seen the collapse of Woolworths and many other large businesses, with more on the verge.

Energy and environmental crises, banking and currency instability, the fear of terrorist activity and many other factors are making life harder for entrepreneurs. Add to that the proliferation of marketing messages that assault every one of us every day and you begin to appreciate the size of the challenge.

Naturally, marketing is not the only factor determining business success or failure (some of those failures never got past step one). However, no matter how good your product or service is, if you don't reach your potential customers and make it clear how your business will benefit them, your other efforts will be for nought.

Time saver

The best way to save time is to benefit from the knowledge of those who have already done what you are setting out to do. You'll find information on all phases of entrepreneurial success in the other books in this *For Entrepreneurs* series, including *How to Start Your Own Business for Entrepreneurs*, *How to Grow Your Business for Entrepreneurs*, *Selling for Entrepreneurs* and *Book-keeping and Accounts for Entrepreneurs*.

David is the new Goliath

One thing that prevents many entrepreneurs from giving marketing their attention is the fear that they will not be able to compete with the bigger businesses in their realm. But, as marketing guru Seth Godin said in his book of the same name, 'small is the new big'. Journalist Janet Rae-Dupree documented this in a *New York Times* article in August 2008. She pointed out that back in the late 1990s it was the goal of most small start-up companies to get big as quickly as possible. These days the trend is in the other direction. Big businesses are finding that the way to foster innovation is to break large business units down into smaller chunks that can operate with fewer layers of bureaucracy and respond more quickly to changing market conditions.

If your company is a small to medium-sized enterprise, you already have this advantage, and you can make the most of it by involving your employees in the innovative marketing methods you'll find in this book.

> ## If size did matter, the dinosaurs would still be alive. WENDELIN WIEDEKING

Marketing Hall of Fame

Reggae Reggae Sauce

An example of a business that started as a minnow and is rapidly becoming a whale is Reggae Reggae Sauce. It's a Jamaican jerk spice created by Levi Roots. He made it in his kitchen and sold it at the Notting Hill Carnival. His big break came on the BBC show, *Dragons' Den*, where Roots convinced investors Richard Farleigh and Peter Jones to put up £50,000 in exchange for 40 per cent of his company. The dreadlock-wearing chef/inventor won them over largely on the basis of his lively and appealing personality – he came on singing the 'Reggae Reggae Sauce' song, which was later released as a download and CD to benefit Comic Relief.

The product is now carried in various supermarket chains, including ASDA, Tesco, Waitrose and Co-op. It sold more than half a million bottles in the first three months, becoming Sainsbury's fastest selling product. Roots has since developed more food lines with the same brand, as well as a television cooking show.

While the product is tasty (I've tried it), the key to its success is having a larger than life frontman and, of course, fortuitous television exposure. For some businesses, having such a spokesperson can be a very effective marketing tool. It doesn't always have to be the founder, either. There may be an employee, like Halifax's Howard, who is better suited to the role. You can even use a puppet or a cartoon figure – for instance, for many of us Tony the Tiger will always be associated with Kellogg's Frosties. He first appeared in an advert in 1952 and continues to this day, demonstrating how long a mascot can thrive if the public warms to it.

Do what the competition doesn't

The good news is that most entrepreneurs are simply not very good at marketing their businesses – good news for you, that is, if you learn how to excel in this arena. Often your competition will be people who are great at coming up with new ideas, who love the challenge of getting a business on its feet and whose enthusiasm carries them into the marketplace. But frequently they fail to appreciate how important it is to *actively* and *continually* reach out to potential customers in a dynamic, flexible and effective way. Typically they fail to measure the effect of their marketing efforts and rely on intuition rather than facts.

The other thing that many marketers forget, even though it has been the acknowledged foundation of marketing and sales for many years, is that we buy based on emotion and then use logic to justify our decision. That means your marketing must address the feelings as well as the intellect of the potential customer, using the power of storytelling and the principles of psychology that you'll read about later in this book.

More evidence that we buy based on emotion.

"The salesman told me this toupee would make me a babe magnet."

Focus: the secret of successful marketing

Strip away all the jargon and the sometimes mystifying statistics, and marketing is a skill like any other and, like any other, can be learned. Robert Middleton, owner of Action Plan Marketing, points out that most people market themselves in a haphazard, unfocused way and that successful marketing takes real intention. This means knowing what you want to produce and why, what your plan is, what the obstacles are and how you will overcome them. He says, 'This kind of clarity of intention and focus can produce extraordinary results.'

In these pages you'll find out exactly how it is done, with case studies and interviews featuring some of the most effective marketing experts there are – people who have been there, done it, and done it well.

A quick tour of the rest of the book

You can read through this book from front to back or you can dip into the chapters that you think are most relevant to the challenges you are facing today. To help you decide, here's a quick guided tour through the chapters that follow.

Chapters Two to Five complete the section on the marketing mindset. Chapter Two starts with a quick quiz to measure your own marketing mindset and then explores the ten beliefs that characterise an effective marketer. You may find you are already totally in tune with these ten principles, or you may find one or two of them are new to you. Either way, being sure that you have the right mindset is an excellent way to start.

Chapter Three shows you how to find the thing that sets your business apart in the minds of your potential customers. This USP ('unique selling proposition') is vital in today's crowded marketplace. No longer is it enough for what you offer to be pretty good or inexpensive. Customers are becoming more discerning, and in this chapter you'll see how a number of companies have distinguished themselves. Their examples will inspire you to identify your own USP if you haven't done so, and to ensure that, if you already have one, it is strong enough to put you in a powerful position.

In Chapter Four we'll look at different marketing segments, and by answering a brief series of questions you will be able to identify the niche you are targeting. You will also get tips on how to find out where those particular people are to be found, so that you can deliver your marketing messages efficiently and effectively. The chapter also includes case studies of entrepreneurs who made their fortunes by cultivating a niche market.

Chapter Five explains how your USP relates to branding and outlines the methods available to you to let customers know just how good you are and why they should be dealing with you. It covers the best practices of public relations, explained in an interview with PR professional Amanda Barry-Hirst. You will find out how to write effective press releases, as well as the dos and don'ts of publicity stunts. Again, these concepts will be illustrated with a variety of case studies.

Chapters Six to Eleven identify your marketing toolbox. Storytelling is a brilliant marketing mechanism and you'll find out how to do it in Chapter Six. The star of the chapter is the Hollywood 'hero's journey' formula, which works brilliantly not only for blockbuster films but also for marketing messages, whether in the form of adverts, sales letters or pitches and presentations. You'll also discover the mistakes many entrepreneurs make when formulating a message, as well as how to avoid them.

Chapter Seven covers the marketing opportunities that come with new media such as blogs, podcasts and email. In this chapter you'll find out about permission marketing – the approach that allows you to create a relationship of trust with your customers and build their lifetime value to you. You'll also find out what to do when things go wrong – for instance, if a competitor uses the internet to disparage or undermine your product or service. Additionally, it reveals the heightened power of endorsements, testimonials and risk-reversal in new media.

The new media may be getting all the glory but there's still plenty of life left in the old media as well, a fact that lots of entrepreneurs are missing. In Chapter Eight you'll find out about the best use today of traditional media, including newspapers, magazines, radio, local television and direct mail. You'll also read a couple of case studies of how successful entrepreneurs are combining new and old media for maximum profit.

Very few entrepreneurs actually test the results of their marketing initiatives on an ongoing basis. Chapter Nine reveals how to do this inexpensively – for instance, with split testing and pay-per-click ads.

If you love to network and are brilliant at it, skip Chapter Ten. However, if you'd rather have your fingernails pulled out than go to one more networking event, or you simply need some tips for improving your technique, then this is the chapter for you. It explains how to make such events palatable and how to exploit newer opportunities for virtual networking using social and business websites such as LinkedIn, Facebook and MySpace.

If you suffer from the 'I'd Rather Do It Myself Syndrome', Chapter Eleven will come to your rescue. The idea of this book is not for you to take on all aspects of marketing yourself, but rather to understand the process fully and know how to manage it. For many small and medium-sized businesses outsourcing a lot of marketing functions is an attractive option, especially by using online services like Elance, Guru, RentACoder and others. They will all be described fully in Chapter Eleven.

Finally, Chapters Twelve and Thirteen show you how to put it all together. In Chapter Twelve you will use all of the information you have gathered in the exercises in the previous chapters to create a one-year individual marketing master plan. You will have specified who your target customers are, what benefits you will offer them, what stories you will use to get this message across, which media to use and so forth. The chapter provides a fill-in-the-blanks exercise that you can accomplish in an hour or less.

In Chapter Thirteen you will find out how to break down your one-year master plan into six-month, three-month, one-month and weekly marketing goals, objectives and activities. The result is a simple, easy to use tool that enables you to track your own efforts as well as the activities you choose to outsource.

More features

Sprinkled throughout the book you'll find some Marketing Hall of Fame entries for marketing efforts that have been unusually successful or noteworthy, and some Marketing Hall of Shame entries for ones that have, sometimes in an amusing way, been more questionable or less successful. You'll also encounter quotes that inform or inspire; Danger! signs of things to avoid or at least consider carefully; Time savers that can help you to work efficiently and effectively; and suggestions for your Toolkit, namely software, blogs, podcasts, websites and other resources to make marketing easier. Additionally, I'll describe some of the web bonus material you can find on the website that accompanies all the books in the *For Entrepreneurs* series. The website address is **www.forentrepreneursbooks.com**.

The first 11 chapters all end with a Marketing power boost – a beyond-the-call-of-duty, out-of-the-box, do-something-different strategy that few, if any, of your competitors will be following – and a Next steps box, in which you can jot down the next actions you will take in order to apply what you've discovered in that chapter.

You have a friendly coach

I hope you can see already how this book will be like a friendly coach by your side as you master the ins and outs of marketing. I'm honoured to help you on your journey as you enjoy working out how to make sure the world will know how it can benefit from your terrific products or services.

Marketing power boost

What do you want to learn?

The first step to wisdom is knowing what we don't know. In that spirit, jot down below six to ten specific things that you'd like to find out about marketing your business. Explicitly stating them will make the information stand out when you encounter it in this book.

_____

_____

_____

_____

_____

_____

_____

_____

_____

_____

Key points

→ Many businesses that offer a good product or service fail due to
poor marketing.

→ Marketing is a skill – you can learn it.

→ Small companies have the advantage of flexibility and these days
can be marketed as effectively as large ones.

→ Marketing must be focused and consistent.

Next steps

What action will you take to apply the information in this chapter? By
when will you do it?

_____

_____

_____

_____

Do you have a powerful marketing mindset?

Chapter Two

Effective marketing begins with having the correct mindset. Your attitudes and beliefs about marketing will colour everything you do – for better or for worse. The good news is that the qualities that have already drawn you to being an entrepreneur are the same ones that you will need to be a good marketer. Probably you have all the essential qualities, but you just may not have worked out yet how they relate to marketing. If you don't have a marketing mindset, you can acquire one. Let's start with a quick quiz on how you perceive marketing.

Your marketing mindset quiz

Circle the point for **a**, **b** or **c** as the best way to complete each statement.

1 The purpose of most marketing messages should be to:

  a explain or demonstrate the unique features of your product or service to potential customers;

  b explain or demonstrate how potential customers will benefit from using your product or service;

  c explain or demonstrate how your product or service is different from what the competition is offering.

2 The most marketing effort should be put into:

  a promoting the part of the business that is weakest;

  b promoting the values and reputation of your company;

  c promoting the part of the business that is bringing in the most revenue.

3 The best time to conduct a marketing campaign is:

  a when you have time in between your other responsibilities;

  b at all times, as a normal part of your business;

  c when you have been able to plan a new campaign fully and in detail.

4 The people who you should listen to when planning and executing your marketing are:

a everybody;

b marketing consultants and other experts;

c your customers.

5 In order to make an impression on potential customers, the best thing to do is:

a copy what your competitors are doing but try to do it a bit better;

b find a way to make your marketing campaign different from the others in your field;

c find one medium you like and stick with that.

6 Testing your marketing campaign is best done:

a continually;

b once a year;

c whenever you start a new campaign.

7 When some aspect of your marketing is not working, the most important thing is to:

a change it as quickly as possible;

b put more resources into making it work;

c learn from the failure and apply the lessons.

8 When some aspect of your marketing campaign is working very well, the most important thing is to:

a protect it by registering trademarks for the catchphrases, characters, designs and so on that you're using;

b work out why it's successful and apply the lessons;

c make sure you don't keep it going so long that potential customers get bored with it.

9 When a marketing campaign isn't going as expected, you should:

    a reconsider your goals for it;

    b invest more time and money in expanding it so that it can have more appeal;

    c stick with your goal but explore other ways of reaching it.

10 If marketing is not something for which you have much feel or interest, you should:

    a read about and study it until you become an expert;

    b learn enough so that when you outsource it you'll be able to tell whether or not the people doing it for you are doing a good job;

    c not worry at all and let the experts get on with it.

The ten principles behind a powerful marketing mindset

Each of the questions in the quiz relates to one of the ten principles that make up a powerful marketing mindset. We'll take a look at these now, although many of them are covered more fully, with lots of examples and specific instructions, in the rest of the book.

1 It's all about benefits

Your product can have all kinds of unique features that set it apart from the competition, and as an entrepreneur it's natural for you to be proud of those and be inclined to make them the centre of your message. But unless you relate those features to what the customer is going to get out of dealing with you, they won't mean much. That's why **b** is the best answer for question one.

There is one thing most of us have in mind most of the time: WIIFM? What's in it for me? If I buy your product or avail myself of your service, will it make me more attractive or give me a way to make more money or make some difficult task easier?

> **Quality in a service or product is not what you put into it. It is what the client or customer gets out of it.** PETER DRUCKER

Later in the book we'll look at the main reasons people buy. The one thing that underlies every buying decision is personal benefit. Even if you convince me to give money to your charity, for instance, it will be at least in part because I get the benefit of feeling good about myself, as well as helping a hungry child or saving an endangered species.

Related to this topic is the changing nature of the relationship between businesses and customers. The more that customers feel harassed by the influx of seemingly endless commercial messages that assault them via a variety of media, the more important it is that you establish a relationship in which potential customers actually want to hear from you. This 'permission-based' type of marketing is something we will explore in greater detail in Chapter Seven; for now, it's just useful to remember that when you can be clear about what's in it for the customer, they will be likely to welcome and even invite your marketing messages.

2 Take advantage of the Pareto principle

Maybe you've heard of the Pareto principle, also known as the 80/20 rule. It states that 20 per cent of our efforts yield 80 per cent of our results. That may sound surprising, but there have been a number of studies of how people spend their working day and generally the consensus is that of the eight hours we spend at work, only about 90 minutes are actually dedicated to highly productive tasks. Similarly, when businesses that sell a range of products analyse where their profit is being made, often it's about 20 per cent of those products that account for the majority of the profits.

In terms of marketing, the Pareto principle is the reason that, generally, it's wisest to put more effort into promoting the products or services that are already a hit with your customers (answer **c** in the quiz) rather than to try to buck up weak parts of your product line. This is counter-intuitive because our first impulse might be to try to improve sales of a product that is not so successful (answer **a**). However, putting money and energy into a flagging product often can only raise it to mediocrity, while putting more marketing muscle behind a success can boost it into becoming a super success.

Danger!

One of the most common marketing mistakes is to keep putting resources into pushing a product or service that customers *ought* to want but that they're not buying. The only expert on what customers really want are the customers themselves and the only proof is when they hand over the cash.

Answer **b**, putting money into promoting your company's values and reputation, often is referred to as vanity marketing. Generally it's not a good use of your resources, although there are some exceptions. For instance, if your product is helping to save the environment, then making customers aware of that can be a plus because it will make some of them feel virtuous for buying it. However, this usually is secondary to some other benefit that the product gives to customers.

3 Conduct an ongoing campaign

If you have read the first chapter of this book you probably selected answer **b** as correct. If you market only when you have time in between other duties, in all likelihood you will never have enough time left over to do it justice.

If you market only when you introduce a new product, you may see your existing products gradually fade from the awareness of potential customers. Yes, the introduction of a new product or service can be a good time to start a new campaign and can for a while dominate your marketing budget, but the only way to be successful in marketing is to make it a constant and consistent part of your business.

4 Listen to everyone

It may surprise you that I recommend you listen to everybody (answer **a**). However, I'm not saying that you will do everything that everyone suggests, only that you begin by listening to everybody. One of the greatest champions of this was Walt Disney. It has become part of Disney folklore that in creating Disneyland he solicited the opinions of all his employees, from the caretakers up to his most senior executives. He once said, 'We don't allow geniuses around our Studio,' meaning that everybody had something to contribute, not just the acknowledged experts.

Here are two more examples:

→ San Diego's El Cortez was the first hotel to have a glass lift built on the outside of the building. Where did that idea come from? Some accounts say it was a bellboy who suggested it to architects and engineers as an alternative to the mess and expense of the traditional approach of chopping a hole down the entire length of the building.

→ Dave Woodward, chief executive of Heinz's UK and Ireland operations, instituted a 'Dragons' Den' event where staff could present their ideas for new products. One of the outcomes was its 'hidden veg' range for children who don't like vegetables – the veggies are blended into the tomato sauce so that fussy eaters don't even know they're eating them.

Great ideas can come from staff or customers. That's why answer **c** is not wrong – it's just not comprehensive enough. In later chapters we'll look at some of the methods for finding out what your potential customers want and how to apply that information to making a success of your marketing.

Toolkit

If you have a list of your customers and their email addresses, one quick way to get input is to ask them to complete a brief online survey. A great tool for this is Survey Monkey (**www.surveymonkey.com**). The website shows you how to design your survey, collect responses and analyse the results. Up to 100 responses per ten-question survey are free, or you can upgrade to a professional subscription that allows an unlimited number of questions and up to 1,000 responses per month. It's a good idea to keep the survey short and to offer an incentive for people to respond. For instance, you might give every respondent a free report, or give a prize to someone chosen randomly from the respondents.

5 Make an impression by being different

The marketplace is getting so crowded that in order to make an impression it really pays to do something different (answer **b**). Just trying to be a little better at marketing than your competitors is not likely to have the major payoff you're looking for. Fashion designer and mogul Tommy Hilfiger told *Ad Age* that if you're going to do something from a marketing angle, 'uniqueness attracts the eyeball. And a different point of view helps you build and create a niche ... We say when the competition zigs, we want to zag.'

Naturally the 'different' should be congruent with your product and your message, not random zaniness or weirdness. Your image should match the nature of your business or you will only confuse people.

In an earlier book, *Do Something Different*, I collected 100 case histories of individuals and companies that found creative (and usually inexpensive) ways to set themselves apart. In each case, their starting point was the message they wanted to send about the benefits of their products or services. The creativity came in the methods they used to get their messages across. For instance, a coffee shop created a little soap opera called 'Days of Our Latte' and posted new chapters on a board periodically. The customers got hooked and dropped in to see how the story was progressing, as well as to enjoy their double espressos or cappuccinos. Instead of sticking with one medium, the most creative entrepreneurs are open to using whatever means and methods they can think of to come to the attention of prospective customers.

It's important that your image matches your business.

Mr. Franklin McGruder
Children's Entertainer

* hilarity
* fun
*spontaneity

JWOLFF

Marketing Hall of Shame

I am rich!

When Apple started allowing the sale of outside applications for its iPhone, one that appeared was a downloadable image of a ruby red gem. The download cost $999.99 – the highest price Apple allowed for any application. It did … absolutely nothing. The gem glowed on the screen, telling anybody who spotted it that the owner of that particular phone was rich enough to spend this amount of money on nothing. Eight people bought it before Apple decided it was not an appropriate product and banned it. Two of those eight ordered it by mistake, assuming it was a joke, and had their money refunded. Of course, it's arguable whether this product is any different from wearing an expensive diamond or a Rolex instead of a Timex, but for sheer pointlessness it does seem a new low in recent marketing history.

6 Test continually

There's a famous quote in advertising that 'half of my advertising money is wasted – the problem is, I don't know which half.' These days there are enough ways to test advertising and every other aspect of business for you not to be in the dark about what's working and what isn't. Furthermore, testing offers you a way to *continually* try out new solutions in order to keep improving, even on what's working well already (answer **a**). As with marketing itself, testing is not something to do once in a while or only when introducing a new product or service – it should be done all the time. In Chapter Nine you'll discover specific methods of testing that are inexpensive and easy for the entrepreneur to use – you don't need to be a statistician or mathematician.

7 Learn from failures

When you're trying lots of different things, it's obvious that some will work better than others, and some may not work at all. So what should you do when a particular marketing campaign or method is failing? You might have answered **a**, change it as quickly as possible. Certainly you don't want to throw good money (and time) after bad. However, probably **c**, learn from the failure and apply the lessons, is an even better answer. Rather than just distancing yourself from the failure, take the time to analyse what went wrong, because that learning will help to ensure that you do not repeat the mistake. The idea that 'there is no failure, only learning', may sound naïve, but there is a lot of truth to it. As you know, most successful entrepreneurs have some big failures in their past, and it may be that what sets them apart is their willingness and ability to learn from those failures and keep going.

8 Learn from success

It's just as important to learn from success as from failures (answer **b**). While you should take reasonable measures to protect your intellectual property, there will always be people trying to copy success. However, if you can work out what it is about the campaign or technique that is really making it a success, you can stay one step ahead of the competition by applying it again, perhaps with a variation. While competitors are busy copying you, you will be working out how to apply these lessons of success to whatever you do next.

If you answered **c**, make sure that you don't keep a successful message or technique going so long that potential customers get bored with it, you should be aware that it is usually entrepreneurs, who tend to have a big appetite for variety, that get bored long before customers do. If a method is still working and has not been diluted too much by imitation, stick with it.

9 Stick with your goals but be flexible

When things are not going as expected, the best strategy is to stick with your carefully thought-out goal, but to explore other ways of reaching it (answer **c**). Sometimes we get so caught up in the means to an end that we confuse it with the end itself. If you have a product that you know has appeal for students, for instance, but your campaign to reach them using radio adverts isn't working, the lesson is not necessarily that you were wrong to try to reach that audience. It may simply be that you need to brainstorm other ways of reaching them. For example, the hugely successful energy drink Red Bull created demand by giving away samples at university events, dances and clubs, rather than advertising in student publications or on pop radio stations. Trying to reach a similar target group, Toyota didn't run ads for its Scion brand initially, but parked the car near graffiti parties in New York and sponsored a dance club event at which it distributed a Scion magazine and free Scion CD sampler. Often it is not more money or time that is called for, it's more creativity.

10 Know when to outsource

When you've finished reading this book you will have a pretty good idea of how much you want to conduct your company's marketing efforts yourself. It may be that you get excited about the process and can't wait to get started. Or you may decide this is not an arena that you have a feel for or would enjoy. If it's the latter, at least by having read the book and having a look at our associated website, **www.forentrepreneursbooks.com**, you will have done what was suggested in answer **b** – learned enough about marketing so that when you outsource it you'll be able to tell whether or not the people handling it for you are doing a good job. That's preferable to assuming that the experts automatically are doing everything right or that it makes sense for you to spend your valuable time trying to develop expertise in an arena that doesn't interest you.

If you take these ten principles on board, you will have the marketing mindset you need in order to succeed. Later chapters cover many of these principles in greater detail and give you specific, practical methods for using them to make the world aware of what you are offering. In the next chapter we'll consider the crucial question of what makes your business unique.

Marketing power boost

Learning from the masters

Once a week, by yourself or with members of your staff, select a business that you admire or that has had outstanding success. This doesn't have to be a business in your field – indeed, it is better if it's not. Dedicate 20 minutes to dissecting the success of this business. List the key attributes that make it work. Then spend another 20 minutes brainstorming how you could adapt those methods to what you do. For example, one of the methods that McDonald's uses is asking automatically for an additional sale ('Would you like fries with that?'). How could you adapt that to your business?

Web bonus

At our website, **www.forentrepreneursbooks.com**, click on the 'Marketing for Entrepreneurs' button. On the link for Chapter Two you'll find three case studies of entrepreneurs who profited by doing something different, as well as ways to apply their methods to your business.

Key points

→ Effective marketing requires the correct mindset.

→ The key thing customers care about is how your product or service solves their problem.

→ To make an impression, do something different.

→ Testing is vital, so that you can do more of what's working already and adjust or abandon what isn't.

Next steps

What action will you take to apply the information in this chapter? By when will you do it?

_____

_____

_____

_____

Why should they pick you?

Chapter Three

You have probably heard of the term USP – or 'unique selling proposition' or 'unique selling position'. It refers to whatever makes you different from and better than the other options people have when deciding between products or services. If you don't have any unique qualities then you will have a very difficult time competing in the marketplace. However, it's very likely that when you were inspired to start your business, you had in mind something special to offer to customers that they can't get easily from your competitors. This chapter will help you to clarify your USP or, if you don't have one, to invent one.

The reason must be compelling

'We do things pretty well and don't charge the earth' is not a USP. It might have been enough to allow a business to survive a few generations ago, when a town or neighbourhood had only one butcher, one greengrocer, one chap who repaired things, one newsagent and one clothing shop. Nowadays, you are not only competing with big chain stores, but you are also up against competitors on the internet who may be located in the next city, the next country or even the next continent. Consumers have a lot of choice, and seeing that you're not too bad at what you do and that you charge pretty much the same as everybody else isn't a compelling reason for them to come to you.

The dangerous USP that entrepreneurs sometimes try is 'cheaper than all the rest'. There are two problems with this strategy. One is that you may quickly find yourself being undercut by a competitor – even if only for long enough to drive you out of business. The other is that customers who base their purchases solely on price are, by definition, not loyal. At the first hint that someone else can save them more pennies or pounds, they'll be off.

Fortunately, you have many options for coming up with and communicating a compelling USP. To gauge where you are now in terms of a USP, please jot down your answer to this question: What is the single most attractive or appealing thing about your product or service?

You'll notice that I haven't left a lot of space for you to write your answer. That's because a good USP can be summed up in a phrase or short sentence. If you tried to cram in three or four sentences, try again – this time boiling it down to one:

_____

Does your statement talk about features rather than benefits? If so, rework it so that it's about the latter. For example, let's say your product is a soft drink. You might be inclined to say that your USP is that 'Lemo-Spritz has no artificial additives'. That's great, but what benefit does that feature give me? A better statement would be: 'All-natural Lemo-Spritz doesn't pollute your body with additives'. Don't leave your customers to work out the benefit – spell it out for them. If you can think of a way to make your USP more clearly about benefits, rewrite it here:

_____

Questions to help you clarify your USP

If you're still unclear about your USP, here are some questions that might help:

→ When you started or bought the business, what was the one thing about it that excited you the most?

→ When you tell people about your business, what do they find most interesting about it?

→ If you were suggesting to someone that they choose your business over all the other alternatives, what's the one most convincing reason you could give them?

→ Among your satisfied customers or clients, what's the one thing they compliment the most?

Somewhere in those answers is your USP – unless your product or service doesn't offer anything different or unique, in which case there is no time to lose in modifying it. Or you may find you don't need to change anything other than the way you are presenting or characterising the product so that people see it in a new light.

"I used to know Jack's USP, but I've forgotten it."

Marketing Hall of Fame

Black is the new black

LCD television screens have recently gained ascendancy over plasmas, but Pioneer believes that its sets have a strong USP: they produce deeper blacks than LCD televisions, especially in dim light.

To call attention to this feature, the company hands out black pens, black press kits and black shopping bags at press events. Even its executives' business cards are black. At one press event the company took over a flat in which it allowed the press to compare its TVs with a variety of competing LCD sets – and named the setting the Kuro Loft (Kuro means black in Japanese).

It's a good example of how to reflect your USP in just about every aspect of your marketing.

USP examples: beyond Starbucks

Starbucks is often cited as an example of a business that gained its success by creating the USP of being a 'third place' to enjoy coffee (home and your office being the first two). The idea is that in this third place you don't have the pressures and distractions of the other two. But what about the other coffee chains? What can they possibly do to set themselves apart? In *Business 2.0* magazine, writer Georgia Flight discovered the competitive strategies of five rivals to Starbucks: emphasising 'green' credentials (Green Mountain Coffee Roasters), constant innovation in product offerings (Coffee Bean & Tea Leaf), going into foreign markets like India and adapting the product to local tastes (Costa Coffee), going upmarket (Peet's Coffee & Tea) and selling an adventure lifestyle through decor (Caribou Coffee).

The danger of being too different

Being different is good, but if you are *too* different it can cause problems. Brad Barnhorn and Tom Hicks came up with a tablet that dissolves in water to create a vitamin-rich carbonated beverage. Hicks told *Entrepreneur.com* that when they first presented it to buyers, the response was: 'We buy beverages. We don't buy pills.' Barnhorn noted that while you want to look to trends in order to offer something different and disruptive, retailers and others that you have to deal with usually have their eyes on tomorrow, not next year. His verdict: 'It's definitely a balancing act.'

That doesn't mean you should give up on products and services that are very different, only that you have to work out how to explain them in familiar ways to your target audience. A famous example is that of Gene Roddenberry, who was unable to sell his series, *Star Trek*, until he described it as *Wagon Train* (a western series that had been very successful) in space.

" **The greatness of art is not to find what is common but what is unique.** ISAAC BASHEVIS SINGER

More USP examples

The following are six further examples of businesses that made the most of their USP. As you read them, see whether they inspire any new thoughts about your own USP.

A super way to exercise

What could be new about exercise tapes? Well, back when supermodel Claudia Schiffer decided to get into that business, her research revealed that women wanted programmes that addressed specific body parts. Instead of making just one tape, she created four, for a programme that women could rotate from one day to the next. 'We were the first to develop this formula,' Schiffer told *Success* magazine 'Since then many exercise videos have followed it.'

Going to the dogs

Dogs these days are pampered just as much as children and some-times even more so. One American franchise that caters to this trend is Camp Bow Wow, a dog day care and boarding service. It provides ele-vated beds with fleece blankets, peanut butter treats and soothing bedtime classical music. The dogs' quarters, called 'cabins', also fea-ture heaters and air conditioners. Greg Powers, vice president of sales and marketing, told *Entrepreneur* magazine: 'We don't refer to our-selves as a kennel. A lot of kennels are very small spaces that are stacked. We don't do that.'

The writing's on the wall – or rather the shoes

Graffiti, or 'tagging', was the inspiration for a new approach to chil-dren's trainers called – naturally – Grafeeti. The canvas shoes are packed in a box that looks like it is made of brick walls covered in tags. The shoes are covered with white strips that can be written on, and the writing can be erased with a fingertip or tissue, similar to a dry-erase board. Children can write slogans, song lyrics, their own names or whatever they want on the shoes and then change it all every day if they so desire.

Child's play

Toy shops have been under a lot of pressure from online competitors, but Eli and Sheri Gurock decided they could compete by opening their Magic Beans toy store in Brookline, Massachusetts. The distinguishing feature? They included a baby section in order to get expectant parents used to visiting the shop before the arrival of their child, to see what a great place it would be to buy toys later. They now have three shops and a website (**www.mbeans.com**), and while their toy sales spike during holidays and Christmas, the baby goods sell all year round.

R U paying attention?

Kids love text-messaging symbols and emoticons (those smiley faces and other symbols on text messages, instant messages and emails), so it only seemed natural to inventor Brian Fried and his company IM:It that they might like clothing, accessories and school supplies featuring them. The brightly coloured items include symbols like LOL (laugh out loud) and GTG (got to go) and are sold in clothing and toy shops.

Playing ketchup

Have you ever gone to a fast food outlet and got tomato ketchup all over your fingers when you tore open one of those little plastic packs? It's a small thing but very annoying, which is why Heinz is introducing new 'peel and dip' ketchup packs.

Ways to create a USP

These examples suggest some of the many different ways that you can create a USP:

→ Like Claudia Schiffer, you can come up with a new *format* for delivering your product or service.

→ Like Camp Bow Wow, you can use *different terminology*.

→ Like Grafeeti, you can *add a new feature*.

→ Like Magic Beans, you can *add a product line*.

→ Like IM:It, you can *take advantage of a trend*.

→ Like Heinz, you can *make your product easier to use*.

If you need a USP, these approaches make excellent starting points for brainstorming the ways to distinguish your product or service. You may already have an aspect that would make a good USP but haven't identified it as such. Notice how each of the examples above focuses on a benefit to the customer, whether that is making the product more fun (Grafeeti and IM:It), easier to use (Claudia Schiffer and Heinz) or higher status so that people can brag to their friends (Camp Bow Wow).

Looking at it another way, each of these innovations solved a problem, even if some of the problems are not exactly high on the list of human needs.

What's your style?

As well as defining your USP, it is vital to define the style and image of your brand. Branding expert John Williams maintains that there are basically three broad image categories:

→ **Flair**: businesses that are associated with creativity, flexibility and friendliness. Typical examples are fashion, entertainment, many retail establishments and companies in the service industry. USPs in line with this include giving customers maximum choice (whether that's what to put on their hamburger or a large number of colour schemes) and making the customer feel at home (for instance, in a pub, restaurant or coffee shop).

→ **Bold**: businesses that are associated with strength, stability and experience. Typical examples are banks, companies in the medical field and some companies in the educational field. Related USPs include providing the most reliable and authoritative advice and safeguarding the customer's money or other assets.

→ **High-tech**: businesses that are associated with technological expertise and innovation. Typical examples are computer hardware, medical devices and communication. Related USPs include increasing productivity or improving the ability to communicate with colleagues or customers.

It is quite likely that you'll have elements of more than one of these styles but that one style will predominate. Once in a while, a business stands out by strongly emphasising a style that is not typical of its niche. For instance, a bank might make a USP of how friendly it is – 'the bank where you are a name, not a number'.

If you are trying to work out the most appropriate style for your business, brainstorm what other product or service in a totally different field is most like it in terms of its essential qualities. Is it trendy and elegant like an iPod? Conservative and reliable like John Lewis? Traditional and friendly like Coca-Cola? Then notice how the business or product you've chosen expresses its style in terms of colours, fonts, advertising, websites and so on, and take inspiration from those.

When you have decided on your style it's vital that all of your marketing materials, such as business cards, letterhead, website and so on, reflect the same tone. Your choice of styles will affect your selection of typefaces, graphics and colours, as well as the wording of your brochures and adverts. If you are outsourcing any of your marketing tasks, be sure that the people doing the work for you understand the style you wish to project.

Danger!

If your USP and your style don't match, it can confuse customers – and confused customers don't buy.

One more time: refining you USP

If you're happy with the last version of the USP you wrote down, stay with that one. Otherwise, take one more crack at making it as succinct and compelling as possible and write it here:

_____

Try out your USP on at least three of your existing customers. Ask them:

1 Does this statement fit our business as you see it?

2 Can you think of another statement that would more accurately describe our business?

3 If our business were able to serve you even better, what statement might reflect how?

Their answers might give you further ideas for refining your USP when you create your marketing plan in Chapter Twelve.

In the next chapter you'll discover how to identify the most promising target audience for your product or service and how to reach them with your marketing messages.

Marketing power boost

Be an explorer

Adopt the 'cool/crappy' notebook strategy of management guru Tom Peters. In his book *Re-imagine!*, he describes it this way: 'On the front cover I wrote COOL. On the back cover I wrote CRAPPY. Then I started recording. Little things.'

As examples of the negatives, he mentioned signage that misleads and software commands that are silly. Among the positives he noted were the thrill of Ziploc bags and the heavenly beds at Westin Hotels. Peters used his notebook to capture good and bad examples of design, but you can do the same with examples of marketing you encounter every day in shops, online and in the media. When you spot something bad, check to make sure your company is not doing anything similar. When you spot something good, ask yourself how you could adopt or adapt it to help you spread the word about your company. If you have employees, encourage them to use a notebook in the same way at least one day a week, and award a small prize every month for the person turning in the most interesting and useful lists.

Key points

→ You need a compelling USP (unique selling proposition).

→ 'Cheap' is not a good USP.

→ Being different is good, but sometimes you need to explain the
unfamiliar in familiar terms.

→ The style and image of your brand are important and should be in
synch with your USP.

Next steps

What action will you take to apply the information in this chapter? By
when will you do it?

_____

_____

_____

_____

Who are your customers and where can you find them?

Chapter Four

Who might benefit from your product or service? Some businesses start with a very specific set of potential customers in mind. If that applies to your business, probably you already have a lot of information about your target audience and where to find them. However, in many other instances, the business starts with an idea or a product that seemingly would appeal to everybody. Unfortunately, if you try to market to everybody, you're making the single biggest and most common mistake of marketing.

Even if it's true that everybody could benefit from your product, there's no way you're going to reach everybody. If you have hundreds of millions of pounds to spend on television and radio ads, you might come close, but I'm guessing you're working with a much smaller budget.

You can't please everyone

One reason some entrepreneurs are reluctant to target their product to a particular niche of customers is that they fear that may alienate other market segments. They're right – but it doesn't matter. Donny Deutsch, advertising expert and host of the *Big Idea* show on CNBC, has strong opinions about this. He says, 'It's better to have thirty-five percent of people really charged up about you and the rest hate you than to have one hundred percent not care.' The goal is to get people to love your product, but it won't be everybody. Donny Deutsch advises, 'Just find the ones who are passionate about it and you'll be on your way!'

By thinking through carefully who to market to, you increase your chances of linking up with people who will be passionate about what you are offering. These are also the people most likely to spread the word about you to other prospective customers. Chapter Five will give you some tips on how to encourage this kind of positive word of mouth.

> **In the modern world of business, it is useless to be a creative original thinker unless you can also sell what you create.** DAVID M. OGILVY

Target market: foodies

One example of a product that was carefully targeted is Good Oil. When Henry and Glynis Braham developed their product, which is created from hemp seed, they were very clear about their likely target customers. 'We knew it was a product for people interested in food ingredients,' Henry told the *Sunday Times*. To get the ball rolling, they sent it to celebrity chefs such as Jamie Oliver and Hugh Fearnley-Whittingstall, whose testimonials were enormously helpful in establishing the credibility of the brand.

In other words

Target market refers to the people you believe will be the most likely customers for your product or service. It can be defined in many ways, including by age, geographical location, interests, economic status, education level or any combination of these.

Describing your target market

There are many criteria that you can use to define who you will target with your marketing. Here are some of the primary ones:

→ **Age**: will your product appeal to children, teenagers, young adults, the middle-aged, the elderly?

→ **Geography**: are you appealing to people in your immediate neighbourhood? Your entire city? Your region? Nationally? Internationally?

→ **Gender**: does your product appeal especially to men or especially to women?

→ **Occupation**: would it appeal to office workers? Builders? Salespeople?

→ **Career level**: would it be something for people looking for their first job, for middle managers, for CEOs?

→ **Hobbies**: would it be of interest to people who like to fish? People who enjoy riding? People who paint in their spare time?

→ **Relationship status**: would it interest singles, people in a committed relationship, people newly engaged or recently divorced? New parents?

→ **Values**: would it appeal to those especially concerned with protecting the environment? Those worried about their personal safety? People wanting to be seen as high status?

Naturally this is not a comprehensive list and you may find that your product or service would appeal to people with some combination of these and other attributes. For instance, a bridal gown business would appeal to women who are engaged, while a new line of expensive high-tech, fishing rods probably would appeal mainly to men who already have that hobby.

Your turn: who are your customers?

Using the criteria above and any others that occur to you, write a brief description of the kind of person who might be a typical customer for your business.

_____

_____

_____

Here is a set of questions to ask yourself to help you define your market further:

→ With whom do I already have credibility and connections?
→ Who is most in need of this product or service?
→ Who will be most receptive?
→ Who can afford this product or service?

If you are marketing to other businesses, you can adapt these questions to work out which types of business to approach, and also the characteristics of the buyers within those businesses.

Target: people who want to be more productive

To make this process clearer I'll use an example from my business. One area that I'm very interested in and in which I have developed expertise is time management. I have a right-brain approach that works for people who have not had much luck with the more traditional methods. My products are an e-book and a related multimedia system. In theory, of course, just about everybody could be interested in making better use of their time, but we know that 'everybody' is not a good target. Applying the criteria above (age, gender, relationships, and so on) doesn't narrow the field too much, so let's see how the new set of questions helps.

1 With whom do I already have credibility and connections?

Obviously it's easier to sell to people who already know you and, ideally, have a good opinion of you. In my case, two groups come to mind. First, freelance writers who know me from my writing-related books and workshops. Second, businesspeople who know me from my business-related books and workshops. I can now answer the rest of the questions with these two possible audiences in mind.

2 Who is most in need of this product or service?

Both groups. Many people do their writing in addition to a full-time job, so managing their time is vital. And businesspeople these days are supposed to be on call all the time and have to balance that with family and social life, so they definitely need help managing their time.

3 Who will be most receptive?

This is always a guess, but in this instance I'd say the writers might be more immediately receptive to my USP ('gain two hours a day by using revolutionary right-brain methods'). However, businesspeople probably are desperate enough to consider doing something different, especially if (as is true for many) they have tried the traditional methods and found them lacking.

4 Who can afford this product or service?

The e-book could be afforded easily by both groups, but the higher-priced system, which includes a workbook, an audio CD and a DVD, probably will be a tougher sale for writers and other artistic types, many of whom don't have a lot of money. On the other hand, businesspeople generally are ready to spend money to make money. If they have seen via the e-book that my system can save them two hours a day they will not balk at paying more for a follow-on product that makes this even easier. Since my bigger profit margin is in selling the system, this is an important deciding factor.

My decision: go for the business niche. It might be a slightly more difficult marketing challenge at first but the greater profit potential makes it worth it.

Your turn: refining your target market

Now take a moment to answer these questions for yourself. Again, they will work whether you are selling directly to customers or to other businesses. If you have already narrowed your appeal down to two or three possible audiences, use the questions to decide which one to give most attention. Jot down your answers below or on a separate piece of paper.

1   With whom do you already have credibility and connections?

_____

2   Who most needs your product or service?

_____

3   Who will be most receptive?

_____

4   Who can afford this product or service?

_____

Based on these answers, what is your preliminary choice of target group?

_____

If answering these questions has changed your idea of your typical customer, write a new brief description of that person here:

_____

_____

_____

Connecting with your customer

There is a powerful method you can use to connect with the world of your customer. It happens in your imagination but the benefits are real. It's based on Neuro Linguistic Programming (NLP), which often is described as the study of how we communicate not only with others but also with ourselves, using our mind/body (neuro) and language (linguistic) in patterns that determine or at least influence our behaviour (programming). It was established in the late 1970s by Richard Bandler and John Grinder, and now has practitioners all over the world.

This exercise may sound a bit strange at first, but in my workshops many originally sceptical businesspeople have said it turned out to be one of the most useful things they had ever done. It entails standing in three different positions:

A   B
                 C

When you stand in position A, you are being yourself – the entrepreneur. Imagine you are facing someone in position B, who represents the kind of customer you want to attract. Imagine what the person looks like, their posture, what they're wearing and so on. It's easiest to do this with your eyes closed. Then, in your imagination, ask them a question or make a comment about the problem or issue that relates to how they could benefit from your product or service.

Walk over to where you imagined them to be, position B, so that you are facing the place in which you were standing previously. Take a moment to get into the character of the customer. Imagine what this person sees, hears, feels, tastes and smells. Be especially aware of their bodily feelings, and you will probably find your posture changes. Then, in your imagination, respond, in character, to what the entrepreneur asked or said.

Repeat this a few times, walking back and forth between the two positions. Imagine this is a real dialogue between you and a customer. Use it to find out their feelings, their doubts, their hopes and their opinions. You are only guessing when you role play, but you may be surprised at how much comes up and how useful it is. As you know, people buy based on emotions, and what comes up emotionally when you are putting yourself in the role of the customer often is the most useful information.

Finally, walk to a third position, C, from which you can see the other two positions, and replay these exchanges in your mind from the viewpoint of a neutral observer. What do you notice about the entrepreneur? About the customer? When you've finished, jot down any insights that came up, any useful phrases, any questions you realised you need to answer in your marketing materials, in fact anything at all that might be helpful. If you do this in a private place, without interruptions, you should find it easy, especially once you've done it a couple of times. However, if you'd prefer some help with this, you can purchase a downloadable audio track that guides you through. You'll find the link in the 'Marketing for Entrepreneurs' section of the **www.forentrepreneursbooks.com** website.

Let reality be your teacher

As you conduct your marketing efforts you may discover that you have defined your market niche too broadly or too narrowly. You may even find that certain people outside your defined niche are turning up and that it makes more sense to market to the groups of potential customers they represent. Although it's a skill, marketing is not an exact science and it's always best to let the reality of the marketplace guide you.

Many entrepreneurs have started by offering one type of product or service, only to find that customers wanted something different from them. In other cases, it was keeping a close eye on the habits and needs of the target group that gave a business ideas for how to extend its brand. For instance, *Real Simple* is a magazine that launched in 2000 with the remit of making women's lives easier. The publishers realised that their readers wanted more content than fits into the magazine, so now they also publish books and special issues and have a weekly TV show, a newspaper column and daily radio segments. The videos on their website offer cooking lessons, beauty demonstrations and much more. Since their readers want to have personal contact with the brand, *Real Simple* also hosts entertainment and cooking events. By listening to what their customers want, the publishers have gone on to create branded home office and desk accessory products and even cleaning supplies. The better they got to know their target group, the more opportunities they discovered to expand the business.

Where are these people?

There's an apocryphal story about the American bank robber Willie Sutton. Supposedly someone asked him, 'Willie, why do you rob banks?' His answer was, 'Because that's where the money is.' Once you have defined who your customers are, next you need to work out where you can find them in order to make them aware of the benefits of your product or service. Many facets of this will be covered in detail in later chapters on networking, using the new media, using the traditional media and testing to make sure that you're reaching the right people effectively. However, to get you started, here are a few questions you need to answer about your target group. If you're not sure of the answer, take a guess and you can always do more research later.

1 What are three print magazines they are likely to read?

_____

_____

_____

Time saver

If you know that your target customers read a particular publication, contact that publication's advertising department. If you tell them that you're considering placing an advert, they will give you a demographic breakdown of their readership that includes a great deal of useful data and will save you a lot of research time.

2 What are three online sites they are likely to visit regularly?

_____

_____

_____

3 What are three types of place they are likely to spend some of their leisure time?

_____

_____

_____

4 What are three ways they are likely to spend their leisure time when at home?

_____

_____

_____

5 When they have a problem, what are three sources of information they are most likely to use? (Examples: ask friends, use a search engine on the internet, approach a local expert.)

_____

_____

_____

If you can't answer these questions, it would be a good idea to ask a few people from your target group. As you proceed with your marketing plan, you'll discover ways to refine your answers and use them to point you to exactly the right marketing methods to use.

"Any marketer who wants to find my Frank won't have a difficult time."

Marketing Hall of Fame

Jonathan Jay, success coach

Jonathan Jay ended up an entrepreneurial success because he worked out how to find the people most likely to be interested in what he was offering. His idea was to provide training for people who wanted to be life coaches. He assembled a mailing list of people who had attended personal development conferences and targeted them with a simple postcard-mailing campaign. He told the *Sunday Times*: 'At the time I had an overdraft of £20,000. I had £145 in cash and spent it all on marketing … We had 500 inquiries from the mailing and when my bank manager came back from holiday he could not figure out how I was £20,000 in credit.' He went on to create a very profitable training academy and eventually sold the business for several million pounds.

This story is an antidote to all the protests that it takes money to make money. Sometimes it takes just *a little* money to make *a lot* of money. Jay admits that he had no idea whether the coaching academy idea would take off when he did the mailing, but with so little at risk it wasn't much of a gamble. When it quickly became clear that he was on to a winner, he scrambled to put together a training programme. It's an example of what is sometimes called the 'Ready-Fire-Aim' approach to marketing. In other words, just try something – even if you're uncertain how it will work out – and then be guided to the next step by the response you receive.

Who are your customers and where can you find them?

Three who found their niche

For inspiration, let's take a look at three examples of entrepreneurs who have been successful at cultivating and reaching niche markets.

Giving kids a boost

After noticing that children often resisted sitting in booster seats at mealtimes, Amir Levin had an inspiration: don't raise the child, raise the chair. He got a design firm to help him develop a plastic booster that attaches to the bottoms of chairs. Knowing that parents of young children would be the target market for the product, he convened a focus group of mothers with children between the ages of one and five. Their feedback was positive so he knew he was on the right track. He also talked to the buyer at Babies R Us and again the response was good. He spent more time making sure the product was safe and eventually came up with the name 'Kaboost' (a combination of Boost and Kaboom).

Levin decided that his target market would be retailers who sell products for children. To find these retailers, he attended the Juvenile Products Manufacturers Association Trade Show in the US. At the show, 75 retailers agreed to carry the product, and since then that number has grown to more than 150.

Movies with a difference

Are you annoyed by how young people check their mobile phones and even send text messages while they're at the cinema? Me too, but obviously we are not the target market that Kelly Rodriques and Paul Schiff are after. Their company, Blowtorch, was set up to take advantage of this trend. They are producing and acquiring short films and low-budget (under £2.5 million) feature films and making them the centre of social networks for college students. That's why Blowtorch signed exhibition deals with 600 cinemas near college campuses across the United States. Visitors to their website will be able to vote on casting and which songs should be used on the soundtracks of Blowtorch productions. According to *Fortune* magazine, 'People in the audience will be encouraged to pick up their cell phones or fire up their laptops to vote [on which short film is best], text each other, and send messages to the producers, all while the show is rolling.' It is proof that what might sound like a nightmare for one niche (people who like to watch films without distractions) can be a dream for others – and maybe the next niche will be cinemas in which a no talking, no texting, no noisy eating policy will be strictly enforced.

Engaging their niche

When the owners of US jewellery chain William Pitt Jewelers realised that competition from the proliferation of mall-based jewellery stores was posing a major threat to their business, they responded by narrowing their niche. They left the malls, changed the business name to Robbins Brothers and focused exclusively on selling engagement rings. One of the brothers, Steve Robbins, told *Entrepreneur* magazine, 'We had to convince the banks and vendors. Everyone thought we were crazy.' One of their principal ways of reaching potential customers is a series of light-hearted radio adverts featuring Steve and brother Skip. They also use several 'do something different' strategies, including giving away wedding planner guides and creating websites announcing engagements and featuring photos of the couples – all for free. Steve calls this 'good karma marketing', and it has been successful, giving Robbins Brothers a 22 per cent share of their market.

Be a trend-spotter

One of the things you need to keep your eye on is the trends that affect the customers you are targeting. There are general trends in society and more specific trends that may affect only one subgroup of customers. An example of a general trend is the ageing of the baby-boom generation, those born from 1946 to the early 1960s. When they came of age and started having babies, that created another bulge in population, sometimes called the echo-boom. Both of these developments are having a massive effect in the Western world and their influence will continue for years to come.

Economic trends

The state of the economy is a very important trend. When times get hard, for example, some luxury products are seen as frivolous. Especially for products at the lower end of the luxury price scale, it's possible to anticipate this and reframe the way the product or service is presented. For instance, 'You're sacrificing a lot, don't you deserve this little treat?' During difficult economic times consumers also tend to stick with the products and services they already know and trust rather than risk spending money on something new. Tough times can be a signal that you should be spending more on marketing to your existing customers than on trying to get new ones. Your marketing messages can reinforce this instinct to stay with the tried and tested.

Technology trends

There are also technology trends that can change entire industries. Certainly the trend towards digital cameras changed the fortunes of Kodak. Although the company analysed the threat of digital cameras as early as 1981, it didn't take the trend seriously enough and probably couldn't imagine a time when most people would just store their photos on their computers and never print most of them. Of course, it was also tough to let go of a business model that was extremely profitable. The upshot was that between 1998 and 2008 Kodak stock lost 75 per cent of its value and shed more than two-thirds of its employees. The company has managed to bounce back with what it calls Kodak 2.0, a popular line of digital cameras and ink-jet printers.

Only entrepreneurs and companies that are nimble enough to stay on top of technology trends survive, and the faster the response the better.

Danger!

When things are going well, it feels risky to take chances in anticipation of changes that have not yet taken effect fully. However, the danger of hanging on to outdated methods or products is far greater.

Demographic trends

Specific trends within a customer category can also cue changes in your business. If today's older people had the same concept of retirement as their parents, the safest investment you could make would be in golf clubs and slippers. But these days many older people stay in their jobs for longer before deciding to retire, and others retire from their first career to work part-time or to start a new business. They don't stay in the traditional aged-consumer ghetto.

If your business has anything to do with computer games, you will be aware that women now play them just as much as men, especially with the advent of games associated with Nintendo's wii. When computer games were mostly 'shoot-em-ups', it probably wouldn't have made a lot of sense for companies whose products appeal mostly to women to pay for product placement. These days, at least with certain types of game, it does make sense and is happening.

Ecological trends

Trends concerning the environment are becoming increasingly important. For example, the highly volatile price of oil and growing awareness of global warming as a reality rather than just a theory is finally beginning to have a major impact on consumer behaviour, not only in travel but also in a variety of contexts. Suddenly the general public have become more aware of how far the food they eat has travelled, the amount of power their appliances consume and the wastefulness of much packaging.

What an expert trend-spotter has spotted

All of these trends have major implications for how your target market behaves, how to appeal to them and where you can reach them. In his excellent book *Hoover's Vision*, management expert Gary Hoover points out some other major trends as follows:

→ The increasing diversity of the population in the United States. This is true in the United Kingdom as well, although with groups of different origin. In the US it is people of Hispanic origin who make up the fastest growing group, while in the UK the biggest recent influx has been from Eastern Europe. In both cases there are major implications for business as well as media and politics.

→ The changing role of women.

→ The increasing diversity of avocations and interests.

Trends can work in your favour

One beneficiary of a change in attitudes is the Smart car. As *Business Week* magazine reported in August 2008, 'For most of its 10-year history, Daimler's Smart car division has had a reputation for making small cars that lose big money … Turns out the Smart may simply have been ahead of its time.' It revealed that, worldwide, Smart car sales were up 57 per cent. The obvious reason for this is the change in the price of petrol, but the article points out that an even bigger factor may be a shift away from being seen driving around in a 'gas-guzzling', polluting SUV.

Trends can work against you

The trend is not always in your favour. For instance, for some time the birth rate in North America and most of Europe has been going down, which wasn't good news for Kimberly-Clark, maker of disposable nappies. The dilemma was how this division of the company could grow despite this trend. It decided to try to create a superior product for which parents would pay more and be motivated to migrate from other brands. The company spent three years researching how to make a superior nappy with less leakage and a better fit. The outcome was Huggies Supreme Natural Fit nappies, introduced in 2006 with great success. Market research firm Information Resources named it the most successful new non-food product of 2007 and estimated that it brought in over $170 million (approximately £100 million) in revenue.

Look at the big picture

There's a saying, 'We don't know who discovered water, but we can be pretty sure it wasn't a fish.' The same applies to trends – if we are caught up in them ourselves, it can be hard to notice that they are happening. (I'm making a distinction here between trends, which are longer term and usually gradual changes, and fads, which are short-lived and much easier to spot.) That's why it is important to be conscious about analysing what's happening in the world, especially in the world of your existing customers and people who might become your customers. The questions that follow will help you to explore these issues. I suggest you try answering them now and repeat the exercise once a month.

1 What's happening in our society today that wasn't happening ten years ago, five years ago or one year ago? (To help you focus you can break this down into new developments in politics, the media, entertainment, technology, religion and consumer behaviour.)

---

2 More specifically, what's happening in the world of my customers that wasn't happening ten years ago, five years ago or one year ago? (Your customers may or may not be affected by the larger trends you identified. There may be micro-trends that affect them.)

---

3 What's my educated guess about what new things will be happening in the world of my customers in one year, five years and ten years? (Ten years is a long time in this context so don't expect to be right, but use it as an exercise to open your mind to possibilities.)

---

4 What are three possible major developments in the next few years in my field, and what are the implications of each of them? (For instance, during the period when house prices were going up and up there were three possibilities for the future: prices would continue to climb, they would level off or they would go down. As an entrepreneur you might have been forced to choose one of these as the basis for your business decisions. However, to be the quickest to respond to actual conditions, it would have been wise to have considered all the possibilities in advance and to have a plan B and plan C in place. Of course, there are many more than three possibilities in most situations, but focusing on three major ones is a manageable way to think about change.)

_____

_____

_____

5 What is the possible impact of these developments on my product or service? (Don't only consider the dangers; also look for the opportunities. For instance, if you are a financial adviser and you anticipate a further major crash in the financial systems, you may find new opportunities in the field of debt counselling.)

_____

_____

_____

6 What can I do today (this week, this month) to help my business take advantage of trends and developments I have identified?

_____

_____

_____

It is extremely rare for entrepreneurs to make the time for these types of consideration. If you do so regularly, it will give you a tremendous advantage over your competitors.

Now that you know who you need to reach and some of the places where you can reach them, and you have some examples to follow, in the next chapter we'll look at the tools that will help you to do just that, notably branding and effective public relations.

Marketing power boost

Your trend-spotter strategy

To become a skilled trend-spotter, save a month's worth of newspapers and by yourself or in a group pick out all the headlines that suggest that some kind of change has taken place or is about to take place. What you're looking for are not only the political and economic ups and downs, although those are useful, but also the social changes in the wind. Anyone who did that over the past few years would have been early to spot, for example, the proliferation of blogs, the increasing interest in all matters green and people's need to economise due to insecurity about jobs and pensions. Make a list of the changes you sense, based on the headlines, and spend half an hour answering these questions:

→ Do these changes suggest any new potential customers for our product or service?

→ Do these changes suggest any new ways our existing customers could use our product or service?

> → Do these changes suggest any new ways we could market our product or service?
>
> → Do these trends suggest any way we could extend our product line?
>
> If you do this at least once a quarter, you will turn into a practised trend-spotter. If you'd like me to run such a session for your company, please contact me via the 'Marketing for Entrepreneurs' button on our website, **www.forentrepreneursbooks.com**.

Web bonus

At our website, **www.forentrepreneursbooks.com**, click on the 'Marketing for Entrepreneurs' button. On the link for Chapter Four you'll find an interview with a marketing expert on how to identify the most promising niche for your business.

Key points

→ If you try to reach everybody, there's a good chance you'll reach nobody. Instead, identify a specific target market that needs and wants your product or service.

→ Find out where these people hang out – that's where you'll reach them with your marketing messages.

→ Let reality be your guide – the marketplace will tell you what people really want (the clue is in what they'll pay for).

→ Pay attention to trends. They are moving more and more quickly and can work for you or against you. Either way, you have to respond nimbly.

Next steps

What action will you take to apply the information in this chapter? By
when will you do it?

_____

_____

_____

_____

You know you're good – how will they?

Chapter Five

Your unique selling proposition or USP is very closely tied to branding. Branding simply means creating an association in the mind of the customer between your business and one or more quality or characteristic. It's easy to identify the USP of strong brands – for example:

→ the Apple brand is associated with cool design and function;
→ Pot Noodle is associated with quick and inexpensive studenty meals;
→ Volvo is associated with safety;
→ Pixar is associated with the best in animation.

These are all businesses with massive advertising, public relations and marketing budgets, so you may think they are not relevant to you. However, it works the same way with small businesses. For instance, there are three newsagents in my immediate neighbourhood. I associate the small one around the corner with friendly service; the one on Tottenham Court Road with a huge selection of magazines; and the one on the next street … well, actually, I don't associate that one with much of anything and probably that's why I almost never I go there.

On a bigger scale, consider what the Sony brand stands for. A typical response may be, 'Uh, consumer electronics that used to be the best but have now been surpassed by Apple, except in televisions where Sonys are still the best – although I hear Samsungs are really good, too.' That illustrates what happens when your brand loses its USP.

You have a brand whether you want it or not

Your customers will associate your business with certain characteristics whether you want them to or not. It's up to you to make sure that what they remember is a positive quality or range of benefits that sets you apart from the competition. If people don't associate you with anything in particular, your business will be part of the huge sea of mediocrity where most businesses can be found.

When you are outstanding the media will pick up on it, sometimes even without any additional effort from you. For instance, Lucy Kellaway writes the 'On Work' column for the *Financial Times*. Recently, one of her columns was headlined, 'When the pen is mightier than the high-tech gadget'. Most of the column was taken up with a story about her favourite pen, a Cross Century II that her husband had been given at a conference but that she had appropriated. Two years after he had got the pen, the clip on the lid came off and Ms Kellaway decided to test what seemed to be Cross's unconditional guarantee and sent the broken pen back to the company. Six days later it came back with a brand new silver lid. In her column she wrote: 'Cross ... your customer service makes me glad to be alive.' She contrasted that with a bad experience with a computer manufacturer. That kind of positive publicity is worth gold and it didn't come from some expensive PR or publicity initiative, just from giving great service.

A logo is not enough

Too often, entrepreneurs put their money and energy into getting a distinctive logo without having a distinctive product or service. Logos and slogans can help distinguish a brand but are no substitute for a genuine USP. However, when you do have a USP, certainly a clever or otherwise memorable logo or slogan can be a great help. Some organisations even 'own' a particular colour within their field, such as red for Coca-Cola in the drinks industry and for Bono's products for charity, green for BP and brown for UPS.

Reaching out to customers

There are many ways you can communicate your message to potential customers. The two main ones are advertising and public relations. The media you can employ are even more varied, and include television, radio, magazines, newspapers, billboards, leaflets, websites, blogs, podcasts, social media like Facebook, public speaking appearances, networking events and many more. Later chapters will go into greater detail about these, but in this chapter we will cover the basics of public relations, the use of publicity stunts and the type of advertising that is most appropriate for small and medium-sized businesses.

Expert interview
Amanda Barry-Hirst on effective public relations

One of the major ways you will present your company and its USP to the world is through public relations. The following interview provides a quick master course in PR from my friend Amanda Barry-Hirst. She is a highly experienced PR pro and the author of *PR Power: Inside Secrets from the World of Spin*, published by Virgin Books with a foreword by Sir Richard Branson. If your interest in the subject is whetted by this interview with Amanda, I suggest you get her book.

Amanda, can you get us started with a simple definition of public relations and how it differs from advertising?

I define public relations as the persuasion business. You are there to persuade other people to your point of view.

Advertising is also about persuasion, but it is absolutely 100 per cent controlled by you. For example, if you are advertising a car you decide what the photography is going to be, what the copy is going to be, where the ad is going to appear and when it's going to appear – you control the whole deal.

With public relations you're trying to get a third party to talk about the car. That's where journalists come in. Public relations is essentially the business of putting your best foot forward and getting other people to tell the story for you. We all might look at an ad for a car and say, 'Wow, that looks like a really great car but I wonder what the reviewers say about it,' and that's where PR really pays off.

Bob misunderstood the advice to hire someone in the persuasion business.

What are some of the key tools of public relations that you use?
I can tell you about six that I consider the essential elements of your PR toolkit. The first one is the press release and photographs that go with it. That's pretty familiar to most people.

Another one is piggybacking, taking advantage of what's out there already. For example, if you're a producer of soft drinks and there is a food festival taking place, it's a good idea to think about how you could tie in to that.

Number three, which actually applies to a lot of different situations, is simply build good contacts. If you have a good working relationship with journalists they will let you know what they are writing about and you can figure out ways to make your story relevant to theirs.

Number four is case studies. If you're a supplier of software systems, for instance, one way of differentiating yourself from the competition is to get a satisfied customer to tell how they've used your product and what difference it's made to them. Case studies are very powerful and are used a lot in trade publications.

Number five is competitions. They are very easy to do. Publications, broadcasters and online sites want something to offer their viewers or listeners or readers, and giving away your product or service as a prize can be a great way of getting some attention.

Number six is testimonials – other people saying how great they think your service or your product is. They don't need to be as comprehensive as case studies, just positive comments. It's a good idea to collect these as you go along, to create a file of any positive feedback you get in the form of letters, emails or comments. Keep them and ask your customers if they will agree to being quoted by name, because a testimonial with a full name and perhaps a job title will be much stronger than one with just initials or just the job description. Testimonials work especially well on websites. Getting audio or video testimonials is even more powerful.

Danger!

Testimonials that have only initials attached (like 'This workshop was great!' – J. W.) are ineffective and create the suspicion that they may be fake.

One of the tools you mentioned is a press release. What makes for a good press release that is likely going to be paid attention to rather than binned? The first key point is keep it snappy. Journalists do not have time to wade through reams and reams of information. When you write a press release think about what the news is, what it is you're trying to say, and get that upfront. If you read any newspaper piece you'll see that all the key facts are in the opening paragraph and that's also what you're aiming to do with the press release.

Don't use fancy fonts or colours or try to make it artistic. Journalists scan press releases quickly to see whether the content is of interest; anything that slows them down will work against you.

Another really important thing is the title, the headline you want to have grab people. Avoid the temptation to be tricky or funny and instead focus on how you can convey the most newsworthy or interesting aspect of your message in those few words.

If possible, limit the release to one page. If you do need to add more background information, this is best put at the end in a 'notes to editors' section, using bullet points to stay concise. If journalists want to find out more they will ring you. Of course, you must always include your contact details, both an email address and a telephone number. If they're working close to deadline, they may want to phone you rather than relying on email.

And finally, pay attention to how the journalist prefers to receive the press release. Most of the time now it's email, so give some thought to what you put in the 'subject' line as this is your first opportunity to hook their interest.

If you have a photo to go with the release, do you attach it to your email message, or just let them know it exists? You can attach it, and you can print it on a sheet that goes with the release to show what the picture is, which is useful for exhibition press packs, or have it on a website so the journalist can go and download it.

Since you're mentioning websites, can you tell us a little about how the new media are being used and how important they are? New media and social media are essential parts of the mix now. It depends on what your product or service is – if you're in the music business or the entertainment business then I think it's especially relevant to you. You need to make it part of your research at the beginning, when you are looking for the best channels for telling your story, just as you'd consider how best to use specialist magazines, the national press, the local press, radio and so on.

I know it's a big topic, so we'll leave it there, and later in the book there will be an entire chapter on how to use the new media, as well as one on how to use traditional media. But it brings me to the question of how much of all this can be done by the individual freelancer or the owner of a small to medium-sized business, and at what point it is important to get help from an agency or a PR freelancer.

When you're considering whether you need to bring in some expert help I think you need to think about how public relations works. It is most effective when it is sustained. Yes, it can work for a launch, but essentially it's a drip, drip, drip process. You are building relationships and by its very nature that takes time. If you bring in someone to help you, their biggest asset is the relationships they already have.

I would suggest that it's a good idea to get some expert help at the beginning so you can map out what you need to do, who you need to contact, what angles would be best and so on. You might also need help writing a press release, because it's actually quite a difficult thing to get right.

Your image, your brand and building awareness that you exist and offer something good is essential, and for that reason public relations isn't a luxury add-on. It should be part of your budget from the start, but of course, if money is tight, you may have to do much of it yourself.

Any final advice for someone who is going to start doing more of this themselves?

Do your homework – find out what your customers read, what they listen to, what they watch. Plan the best way to use the six tools I mentioned at the beginning and commit to continuing your efforts. Don't get discouraged. Sometimes you can write a great press release, spend time with a journalist who gets excited about your business, and it all looks like the result will be a fantastic article, and then at the last minute nothing appears. Sometimes a big news story breaks and takes up all the space or something else happens that has nothing to do with how good the story is. That's just part of the process; you have to realise that you're in this for the long haul and keep at it. When it does pay off, it can make a huge difference to your success, so hang in there and eventually your efforts will pay off.

Writing press releases that get attention

Because press releases probably will form the core of your PR efforts, it's worth spending a bit of time learning to craft ones that get attention. Start once again by thinking about benefits. This time you need to consider how what you are doing will benefit the media and the ultimate consumers, the readers or viewers or listeners. Journalists are looking for stories that are newsworthy and/or entertaining, and the consumers of media are looking to be informed or entertained. Does your story fit either of those criteria? Most press releases don't, and that's why they end up in the bin. Featuring a headline that sounds like it's only an advert is instant death for your press release.

You also have to match the story to the medium. It may be big news to you that you have promoted Jane Bloggs to the position of Assistant Senior Vice President, but in the bigger world it will rate only as a yawn, so sending that announcement to the national newspapers will be a waste of time. However, if you are a producer of widgets, the trade paper *Widget World* may give it a mention.

Unless you're going to be employing a lot of people or otherwise having a major impact, the nationals won't be interested in the fact that you're opening a branch in Slough – but the local newspaper and radio station may well do a story about it.

If you are offering a workshop or an open house, again it probably won't end up on the news pages but it might well get a listing in an events column.

Whenever you are unsure whether or not a story will be of interest to a particular outlet, just imagine for a moment that it is another company making such an announcement and then assess its newsworthiness or appeal. Taking that one step back will help you to be more objective. Then you can also decide which section of the media to send it to.

Here, reproduced with her permission and that of Prologic, is an example of a press release that Amanda wrote:

BUOYANT PROLOGIC TO BECOME PLC
Berkhamsted-based supplier of IT solutions to fashion industry floats on AIM

Berkhamsted-based Prologic, supplier of integrated management IT solutions to household fashion names such as Ted Baker, Paul Smith, Fat Face and Hobbs, today announced its intention to become a plc by joining the Alternative Investment Market in June.

Led by Managing Director Sam Jackson, who started the company 20 years ago this year, Prologic has grown to become one of the fashion industry's most respected and trusted providers of integrated management information systems. The company's advanced Oracle-based software solution, CIMS, which was designed specifically for the fashion industry, provides the technology backbone to fashion retailers, wholesalers, mail order houses and e-tailing operations both in the UK and internationally.

Jackson comments, 'By taking Prologic public, we will be consolidating our already strong market position and opening the way for even greater investment and growth in the future. This means we can continue to do what we do best – providing our customers with IT solutions that are designed to meet their needs, today and into the future'.

The company's ability to continually innovate, yet stay close to its customers' core needs, is seen as one of the secrets to Prologic's extraordinary success in such volatile markets as fashion and information technology. Prologic's latest innovation is the introduction of a Managed Outsourced IT service, which has been adopted by several of Prologic's existing customer base, including Ted Baker, Liberty, Turner Bianca and Hobbs.

/ends.

Notes to Editors:
1. Photographs available
2. First day dealings in Prologic plc shares are expected towards end of [date]
3. Nominated Adviser and Broker is W H Ireland Limited
4. Sam Jackson founded Prologic in 1984. The company became part of Comino plc, a diversified software group in 1996. In 1999, Sam Jackson led an agreed Management Buy Out backed by Lloyds Development Capital.

Here are a few things to notice about this release:

→ There were two contacts with phone numbers for each. This can help if the journalist is working to a tight deadline and needs to reach someone immediately to ask a question or confirm a fact.

→ The headline is succinct and supported by a more detailed subheading.

→ The first paragraph tells who, what and when.

→ The 'why?' comes up in paragraph three, as does a quote from a corporate spokesperson that helps add weight to the release.

→ The short paragraphs make the copy more readable.

→ The final section (Notes to Editors) provides important background information that is clear and easy to find.

Who would be interested in this press release? The most likely interest would be from the financial sections of newspapers and magazines, and that's why the somewhat technical information about the company's background in the 'notes to editors' section is relevant.

Here is an example of a different type of press release that worked well for me:

For Immediate Release
Contact: Jurgen Wolff
[phone number and email address]

Branding Workshop Says Today's Choice for Businesses is 'Distinct or Extinct'

LONDON – [DATE]

'In today's competitive marketplace, you have to make a choice: do you want to be distinct or extinct?' says London-based creativity and marketing guru Jurgen Wolff. For those who want to choose 'distinct,' Wolff is offering a half-day workshop on Saturday afternoon, 1.30pm to 5pm, May 10, 2008, at Regent's College, central London, showing how freelancers and small business owners can create their unique brand. The fee of £99 includes his

---

self-marketing book, 'Do Something Different,' published by Virgin Books with a foreword by Sir Richard Branson.

'Ironically, creative people often are the least skilled at promoting themselves creatively,' Wolff says. The points the workshop will cover include:

- Positioning: how to figure out where you fit into the marketplace
- How to figure out what the marketplace wants from you
- How to get the marketing mindset
- How to figure out your target audience and how best to reach them
- How to create the right image
- How to develop a marketing plan
- How to use a website to promote yourself
- How to use a blog to promote yourself
- How to use a podcast to promote yourself
- Networking success for introverts

This intensive and practical workshop features a series of brief exercises that will allow participants to have a fresh marketing plan by the time they leave the class.

Wolff is a Neuro Linguistic Programming practitioner and certified hypnotherapist, and a successful author with six books and more than 100 hours of produced television to his credit. Based in Camden, he teaches for the Academy for Chief Executives and in private workshops around the world. For more information, see www.timetowrite.com.

For more information or to register for the course, email BstormUK@aol.com or ring Sheridan Bolger on [phone number].

Press contact: Jurgen Wolff – [phone number and email address]. Please contact regarding interviews or photos.

END

Clearly this event was never going to be front-page news. The target for this press release was the editors of listings sections and the features editors of publications that write about business. The intention was that the former would list the date, times, fee and contact information for the workshop, while that the latter might use the 'distinct or extinct' hook to write about the importance of branding. If they did that, the odds are they would quote a variety of experts, but they might make the workshop an element of their article.

Let's look at the components of this release:

→ It features a headline that tells what it's about: a workshop on branding. It also may pique curiosity about the 'distinct or extinct' idea.

→ The first paragraph reveals who the workshop is for: freelancers and small business owners; it also explains the relevance of the 'distinct or extinct' phrase. It gives additional vital information: who, when, where and how much.

→ It then lists the key points of the content (the benefits) bullet-style for conciseness.

→ The next paragraph further describes what will actually happen on the day and adds another benefit: having a fresh marketing plan by the end of the workshop.

→ That's followed by the qualifications of the workshop leader and the address of a website that has more information about him.

→ Next is the 'call to action' – that is, what it is hoped readers will do: sign up or at least ask for more information.

→ At the very bottom the contact information is repeated, and it is made clear that photos are available and the instructor is happy to do interviews.

If you make photos available, it really helps if they are not just the standard head and shoulders, smiling at the camera shots. These look boring on the page. If at all possible, get photos of you doing something interesting at your business or factory, or with a relevant prop. For instance, when I do promotions for my 'tame your inner critic' workshop, I use a shot of me with a little stuffed gremlin sitting on my shoulder – it represents the harsh inner critic that most of us carry around in our minds.

Other format considerations

Here are a few other points that will make your press releases pass muster:

→ Print them on your company letterhead and at the top right, write 'Press Release' or 'For immediate release' or 'Press Information'.

→ Use 1.5 or double spacing and leave generous margins.

→ Use standard typefaces on A4 paper that is white or a pastel shade (vivid paper colours make it harder to read).

→ Use straightforward, easy to read and understand language and avoid clichés or jargon. One otherwise useful guide to writing press releases advises: 'Use words like strategy, vision, enhance, enabling, infrastructure … These are part of business vocabulary and by using them you will give yourself a professional edge.' Nooooo! You will only make the reader's eyes glaze over, which is not a good thing.

→ If your release goes on to a second page, write (MORE) at the bottom of the first page.

→ At the end of the release, type END.

→ When sending the release, fold it so that the contact information and headline are the first thing the person opening the envelope sees.

Where to send your press releases

As mentioned above, it's important to send your releases to the editors most likely to be interested in them. If, for example, your service relates to buying or selling property, then the editor of the property section or supplement is the logical person to target, not the general news editor. Many newspaper and magazine sections list the names of their editors but, if not, you can always ring the publication and ask. You may have some news that could appeal to different sections or different publications. For example, if you are opening a flower shop and are offering free flower arranging lessons during your first week, that could be of interest to both the gardening editor and the editor of the home furnishings and design section of a newspaper. In that case, write two separate releases, slanting each one to the needs and interests of the different sets of readers.

If you are promoting events, be aware of the deadlines for listings columns and for feature stories. Naturally the daily press has the shortest deadlines, whereas monthly magazines may require material three months or more ahead of the publication date (yes, all those magazine Christmas features are written in August). Again, if you are unsure, just give them a ring.

You can also issue press releases via the web. Some services charge for this, while others are free. For up-to-date information on this, see our website, **www.forentrepreneursbooks.com**, or use your search engine to find 'online press releases'.

Being the perfect radio or TV guest

Getting on radio or television is an excellent way of promoting your business. You don't need to be a professional actor or presenter to make a good impression, but you do need to prepare. Here are the things to keep in mind.

Time is of the essence

In most cases radio and TV guests get only a few minutes of airtime. You need to think in terms of 'sound bites'. These are statements that get your message across concisely and in an entertaining manner. For instance, let's suppose you are promoting the opening of a new gym and your interviewer asks you why it is needed. Here are two possible responses that say basically the same thing. The first is accurate but frankly a bit boring: 'Because the rate of obesity is increasing and medical experts have stated that a consistent schedule of exercise can be very helpful in combating this condition.'

The second is the sound bite version: 'Because we're all getting fat, and moving around makes the fat go away!'

They're looking for a hook

That is, an angle that will be appealing to the audience. Most of the time this will relate to your USP. If you are opening a gym, what makes it different from all the other ones out there? Maybe you're offering a new kind of exercise class or classes for kids at the weekends, or you have women-only hours or some new fitness equipment exclusive to you. Without a strong USP, you will struggle to get any airtime.

Keep it conversational

It's not only being brief that's important, it's also keeping the tone appropriate to the medium. If someone is reading a book or article and misses a point or doesn't understand something, it's easy to go back and read it again. On TV and radio if they miss a point they probably will just tune out – mentally or literally. That's why you should avoid citing a lot of statistics or complicated information. Keep it light.

Always be thinking, 'benefit, benefit, benefit'

Remember, people who are listening or watching are thinking WIIFM? ('what's in it for me?'). They may think they're not interested in joining your new gym, but if you offer them three tips for getting more exercise without much more effort they will continue to pay attention. If you can make it entertaining, that's another reason for them to keep listening or watching.

Sell, but don't over-sell

You should mention the name of your business or product but not so often that your interview sounds like a long advert. You've probably heard this rule being violated by authors who start every sentence with, 'Well, as I said in my book (name of book)…' It annoys the interviewer and the audience. If you are being brought on as an expert about something in the news, then don't sell at all. The interviewer will mention your product or business in the context of establishing your credibility and that will be enough.

Be prepared for things to go wrong

Some years ago I was invited to go on a TV show to promote a book called *Help for the Overweight Child*, which I co-wrote with a psychologist whose speciality was helping obese children. The producer and I agreed that a good first question would be why it's easier for children to lose weight than it is for adults. When we were on the air the host put on his best smile and said, 'Let's start with why it's so much harder for children to lose weight than it is for adults.' The challenge was how to correct him without making him seem like he hadn't done his homework. I said, 'That's a great question because it incorporates the number one myth about weight loss for children. As you say, it seems logical that it would be easier for adults, but in fact it's the other way around. The reason is…' Always try to make the host look good, no matter what happens.

Be prepared for a surprise attack

Some shows thrive on controversy and conflict, and if you watch or listen to them regularly you'll realise that and decide whether you really want to be discussing your business or product in that setting. If you decide that you do, you'll be ready to defend yourself. But it's important to be prepared even if the show isn't normally particularly aggressive. One TV show on which I appeared in order to promote another diet book had a guest host who was very sweet to me before the show. She said I should forget all about the camera and just chat with her like a friend. The camera's red light went on, she introduced me, turned to me and said, 'Why on God's earth do we need another diet book?' Fortunately, I had anticipated that someone would ask that question so I did have an answer ready, but the rest of the interview felt like the return of the Spanish Inquisition. When it was over and the camera went off she smiled, patted my knee and said, 'Wasn't that fun?' This doesn't happen very often, but it's best to be ready.

Give the audience a reason to contact you

If the producers will allow it, at the end of the interview offer the listeners or viewers something that will motivate them to get in touch with you. This could be a free booklet, a video on your website or a free sample of something. The BBC will be more resistant to this than local commercial stations, but it's worth a try. At least see whether they are willing to say something like, 'And for more information, listeners can go to your website, www.yourwebsite.com.' If you are offering something specific of use there, it's more likely this will happen. If they won't send people to your website, they may agree to put your contact information on their own site.

Follow up your interview with a note of thanks

This should be to both the host and the producer. Most guests don't do this so it will make you stand out and increase the chances that you will be asked back.

Getting the invitation

The points above also tip you off as to how to get invited on radio or television in the first place. If your press releases are concise and have a strong hook, have a natural and entertaining tone and provide information that is beneficial to the audience – and they indicate that you are available for radio and television interviews – they will do much of the work for you. You can also target a particular show with a letter offering to appear to discuss your area of expertise. If you can tie it in to something topical they will be more likely to pay attention.

Using the 'benefits' state of mind regarding how to make the producer's job easier, one thing that works well is to provide a list of suggested questions or talking points, either in the press release or available upon request. You can also put it in the 'press' section of your website.

If a producer is interested, most likely they will phone you for a chat. No matter how informal this sounds, it's an audition. They will ask you a few questions, and as well as assessing how good the content is, they will be paying attention to how well you express yourself. If you go on and on or get tongue-tied, probably they will not ask you to be on their show. That's why it's good to have a few sound bites ready and to do some role-playing with a friend.

If you are invited to go on the show, the producer usually will be able to tell you how long your segment will be and give you any other special instructions. Listen to the show a few times before going on and take along a card with your key sound bite points on it so you don't forget anything (more easily done on radio programmes, of course). Allow yourself to have fun because that comes through and makes you more enjoyable to listen to as well.

The power of doing something different

One public relations and publicity tool that can get you a lot of attention without costing much money is the publicity stunt. It can also backfire, though, so it's vital to get it right.

The father of the publicity stunt was P. T. Barnum. He is often mis-quoted as saying, 'There's a sucker born every minute.' In fact he was not trying to cheat people, he simply wanted to entertain them, and he realised that playing tricks on people could be entertaining for them and lucrative for him. One of his stunts was to get an elephant to plough some land he owned near railway tracks leading into New York City. Commuters saw this strange sight and talked about it, as did the press. It got Barnum publicity across the United States. In his memoirs he wrote: 'The six acres were plowed over at least sixty times before I thought the advertising sufficiently circulated...'

Publicity stunts continue to this day – and not only in Hollywood. A couple of years ago David Hart found a jar apparently containing a dragon embryo in his garage in Oxfordshire. With the jar was a letter written in the 1890s suggesting that the jar had been in the possession of the Natural History Museum but had been taken by David Hart's grandfather. David Hart happened to own a marketing company (hmm, suspicious), yet the media gave the 'discovery' lots of attention. After the story had appeared in media around the world, Hart confessed that the 'embryo' was a model made by the artisans behind the BBC's *Walking With Dinosaurs* series and had been created to publicise a fantasy thriller novel, *Unearthly History*, written by his friend Alistair Mitchell under the pen name P. R. Moredun. Mitchell admitted, 'I created the hoax in order to attract potential readers.'

What kind of stunts are effective?

When a stunt is amusing, and especially if it has a visual component, the media love it and give it their attention. However, there are a few crucial things to remember.

→ It should be relevant to your product or service. Just as with an advert that people find amusing but can't remember the product it was advertising, a stunt that doesn't connect clearly to your product is a waste of time.

→ It should be congruent with your product or service. People don't expect anything zany from a dentist or someone handling their money.

→ Don't do anything that will humiliate or insult people – one negative quote from a disgruntled person can poison the whole story.

→ It should not be anything that could possibly be construed or mistaken as dangerous. One American company learned this to its cost when, to promote a forthcoming animated TV show, it planted boxes with blinking red lights around Boston. Bomb disposal squads were dispatched, major roads and motorways were shut down – and nobody was amused. These days you have to be extra careful about this.

Dexter's bloody fountains

Marketing Hall of Shame

To promote the television series, *Dexter*, about a serial killer (who kills only bad people, so I guess it's OK…), Showtime turned the water in various fountains in US cities blood red and put up yellow crime-scene type tape around them. They had people in white coats by the sites, handing out free DVDs and hand sanitiser. Sorry, Showtime, but in my view simulating gushing blood in city fountains is a step too far down the ladder of taste.

Another ploy they used, this time in Portugal, was having actors with knives in their backs lie on the pavement. If someone came up to them to see if they were all right, the actors would hand them a flyer for the series.

Sometimes, in the desire to do something different, marketers don't stop to consider whether what they're doing is likely to be offensive or upsetting. While it's true that almost everything will offend someone, certain notions overstep the bounds of good taste. Perhaps the Showtime stunts seem offensive to me because Britain is in the middle of an epidemic of knife crime among youngsters (although, to be fair, neither of these stunts were used in the UK).

Stunts that worked

Publicity stunts don't need to be on the level of elephants and fake dragon embryos. Here are some examples of inexpensive stunts that got attention from the media.

How sweet it is

Headline, the publisher, teamed up with chocolatier Thorntons for a one-month promotion of *The Chocolate Lover's Club*, a novel written by Carole Matthews. Each of the 378 branches of Thorntons gave away a sampler of the book. This sampler, in turn, gave readers a chance to win a chocoholics' weekend away with Thorntons' master chocolatier. The 35,000 members of Thorntons' online site had the chance to win a copy of the book, while Matthews' 20,000 newsletter subscribers were offered a discount for Thorntons products and the chance of winning a hamper of sweets. The promotion was launched at Matthews' local Waterstones bookshop with Thorntons chocolates as the giveaway.

This is an excellent example of a win-win collaboration. Both Matthews and Thorntons got publicity and access to new customers with a great stunt.

Stay a while

Shopping malls in the United States and in Great Britain are facing a major challenge in the form of increasing online sales. With the cost of petrol and the hassle of dealing with traffic and parking, many consumers are taking the easy way out and ordering from the comfort of their homes. 'The challenge that owners and developers face is how to keep that [mall experience] fresh, how to keep people coming,' said Patrice Duker of the International Council of Shopping Centres. One response to this at the Serramonte Centre, in a suburb of San Francisco, was to install a large koi pond and place wicker armchairs, coffee tables and rugs throughout the mall to create homely oases. Tired shoppers can put up their feet and rest or just watch the world go by.

I'll take a consonant

There can't be a much bigger marketing challenge than for an unknown singer-songwriter to get attention for his work. Wimbledon-based young musician Jonathan Haseldon found a way – offering individual lines of his lyrics for sale on eBay. He ran that campaign for four months and, according to the *Guardian*, sold the line 'And when you're lost, you'll always be found' for £11,100. The bidder will get 2.2 per cent of the royalties from the song from which that line comes when the single is released. He did similar deals with TGI Friday's, Taylor Guitars, the Tussauds Group and Budweiser Budvar. Probably more important than the money was the coverage he got not only in the *Guardian* but also from BBC London, the *Daily Mail*, the Canadian Broadcasting Corporation, the *Evening Standard Lite*, GQ.com and many more, as well as an invitation to the music industry's Gold Badge Awards and an inquiry from a Hollywood agent about the film rights. All from an idea that most people probably would have considered silly and unlikely to succeed. (Note that individual sentences of this book can be bought for a mere £1,000!)

Using her (moose) head

Jennifer Wilson owns the Moose Mountain Trading Company, a clothing store in Steamboat Springs, Colorado. Clothing manufacturers provide her with ads featuring perfectly groomed young men and women modelling their jumpers and jackets. Nice, but boring.

Wilson's ad agency decided it would be funny – and a great reminder of the name of Wilson's shop – to put moose's heads in place of the human ones in the adverts. Customers loved it and the campaign was written about in national as well as local publications. Fortunately, even the clothing manufacturers saw the funny side. My guess is that if she had asked them first they would have referred the question to some committee that would have rejected the idea. She was taking a chance by going ahead, but had they objected, probably she just would have had to promise not to do it again. A bit of nerve is very useful for marketers who want to use publicity stunts.

More examples

Here are a further few brief examples, each of which got the business concerned a mention in the *Sunday Times* travel section:

→ London's Cavendish Hotel is arranging instructors from British Military Fitness to give its guests a workout in nearby Hyde Park.

→ Oulton Hall hotel in Yorkshire has a Sunday lunch package in which children will be charged by weight – one pound per stone.

→ The cruise ship *Norwegian Gem* has introduced on-board Botox treatments (with reassurances that the ship's stabilisers will keep things nice and steady).

Getting the word out

Probably the most valuable and least expensive method of promoting your business is via word of mouth. A study conducted by eMarketer.com found that 53 per cent of online traffic was generated by recommendations from friends or family members. When your satisfied customers tell others how great you are and suggest that they also use your product or service, that's the best kind of publicity you can get. Typically this is something business owners only hope for, but there are things you can do to encourage it.

Naturally, before anybody can talk about your business they have to be exposed to it, which is where public relations, advertising and other uses of the media come in.

Sometimes it's a video on YouTube that goes viral and suddenly millions of people have seen the Subservient Chicken or that blender that has been used to pulverise everything from blocks of wood to an iPhone. It's not only videos that blossom that way; it could also be a heart-warming message that people send on to all their friends, a still image that amuses them or stirs them, a useful list of tips, a slide show that inspires them or even just a joke. If whatever is passed along is relevant to your business, and your business name travels along with it, you can gain increased customer awareness almost instantly.

The power of free

Sometimes word of mouth is achieved simply by giving out samples. Red Bull, the hugely successful energy drink giant, did no advertising at the start. Instead the company handed out loads of samples at clubs and parties to the audience it thought would be most receptive – young party types who wanted extra energy for dancing the night away. The fact that Red Bull wasn't something everybody knew about gave it an extra edge with this crowd.

Timing is important

Do you know when people are most motivated to tell others about the benefits of your product? You may be surprised to hear that it's right after they have purchased it. This is part of an unconscious drive to reassure themselves that they have made the right decision. If they can get others to be enthusiastic about their purchase, it reinforces their belief that they haven't made a mistake.

How to get them to talk

Let's assume that you have brought your business to the attention of at least some of your potential customers using the marketing methods described in this book. How do you get them to spread the word? The following are a few options:

→ Ask. Offer them a small reward of some kind – for example, a discount coupon – if they give you the names and email addresses of three friends or colleagues who might also be interested. Position whatever you are giving them as a 'thank you present' rather than a payment or bribe. They want to feel good about spreading the word, not that they're acting like a salesperson.

→ Add a 'tell a friend' button on the order page of your website to take advantage of that post-purchase surge of desire for validation.

→ Create a space for them to talk. Consider adding to your website a forum where your customers can compare notes and ask each other questions. If the discussion is interesting enough they will invite more people to join the forum and the word will spread.

→ This will not work for all products or services, but in some cases by limiting quantities or issuing special editions of a product you can turn it into something the buyer will brag about. This effect can come from artificial shortages as well as genuine ones. In the first days when iPhones were temporarily in short supply, you can be sure that most of the people who got one showed it off to everybody they could.

→ Create a club of some kind and give members valued premiums. Being a member of something that seems exclusive is another ego-booster that people love. Obviously, having a Tesco Clubcard doesn't quite qualify, but having a black American Express Centurion Card does. At the time of writing, for a card issued in the United States, the one-time initiation fee is $5,000 and the annual fee is $2,500 (in the UK it is 'only' £650). There are some excellent perks that come with the card, but how many people find that the principal value is being able to flash it in front of others? If you can give people exclusive membership of a group or club that relates to your product or service, there's a good chance they'll tell their friends and colleagues.

By now it should be clear that your work in coming up with a great USP is the key to getting word of mouth publicity as well. People don't talk much about average products or services. They talk about the unusual and the outstanding.

Marketing for Entrepreneurs

Know what you want them to say

Positive word of mouth is something you should be striving for all the time, but it can also be used when you have a particular message to get across. Your first step is to be very clear about what that message is. It should be something you can easily state in one sentence. Consider as an example the message that I have a big sale coming up that will last for only one week. To relate this to your experience, think of one message that you'd like to have spread about your business:

_____

Your next step is to work out who would be the best people to spread that message. Within your circle of colleagues, friends, customers and strangers, who are the influencers? These are the people others turn to for advice – the ones who go to a lot to conferences, networking events and other places where your message could be disseminated. Or they may have a relevant blog, vlog (video blog) or podcast, a column in a trade magazine or some other way of reaching your target audience. Name a few of the people who fit this description in your arena of business:

_____

_____

_____

If you found this difficult, you need to do some research on who the influencers are in your business world. Start paying more attention to who gets mentioned in your trade publications, who you always run into whenever you attend any relevant events, who has a website, blog or podcast with lots of visitors and so on. In the media, who covers your type of business? Recruit others in your company to help you compile a list and update it every month or two.

Give them something to talk about

Next, you need to give them something that's worth talking about. The mere fact that my company is having a sale, even a great sale, is not enough to get influencers talking. That's where a publicity gimmick can come in, such as the ones mentioned earlier. For instance, let's say my sale is on big-screen televisions. I might set up a blue screen and film customers against that backdrop, and then use a simple special effects programme to make it look like they're flying like Superman or clinging to the side of the Empire State Building like King Kong. I could give them a copy on CD to take home. I would send my local influencers a note saying something like, 'If you'd like to bring your children (or yourself) along and see whether you have the makings of a film star, just give me a ring and I'll book a time so you don't get left out.' With a video camera, a simple blue screen, a laptop computer and the help of a couple of students from my local college, I could create an event that would get people talking and maybe even attract the local media – again, I would suggest they bring along their children to get the special effects treatment. Note that the stunt is relevant to the product. I'm giving people the chance to see themselves on the screens of the televisions I'm selling.

Your turn

What kind of stunt or event can you think of that would make your message worth talking about? Don't be afraid to adapt any of the examples in this book or in my book *Do Something Different*, or ideas you read about anywhere else. If it has worked before, it will probably work again, and there's no copyright on publicity gimmicks or hooks. Jot down your ideas here or in a separate marketing notebook:

_____

_____

_____

Some people love to be first

The key is to let the influencers know about it first. They love to be insiders – to tell people something that they don't know yet. If it's a live event then invite them first. If you have something that you're going to launch on the internet, such as a video, you can send insiders a copy on a CD or DVD first – with a note saying, for instance, if it's amusing, 'Thought you might get a smile out of this.' For my hypothetical special effects event, if I really wanted to catch my influencers' attention, I might ask a graphic design student to make up a personalised invitation on which we have superimposed a photo of the recipient's head on to the body of Superman/Superwoman or King Kong. By using Google Search for images and checking Facebook and MySpace, you will be able to find photos of almost anybody. Failing that, the artist could just draw a blank head with an arrow pointing to it, and write: 'Your head goes here, on [the date of the event]!'

For your idea, what would be the best ways to notify your influencers?

Spread the word even more

Whatever the event or method is, be sure to gather evidence of it that you can recycle into press releases, postings on YouTube and so on. In the case of my sale, I'd take lots of photos or get a photographer to do so, and then post them on our company website and use them to try to get further media coverage after the fact. Naturally, you must always get the permission of anybody in the photos. Get them to sign a standard release form on the day.

It's nice to say 'thank you'

If any of your influencers were especially helpful in spreading the word, be sure to send them a thank-you note, and the next time you have something interesting going on make them the very first to know. If appropriate, send them a small token of your appreciation, like a box of chocolates. This is not recommended for reporters and others whose job it is to cover events, because it smacks too much of bribery. For them, a simple thank you is sufficient.

Warning: WOM works both ways!

One important warning: word of mouth can work against you just as easily as it can work for you. If your events are boring or your videos are not funny or interesting, at best they'll be ignored; at worst, negative word of mouth will get around even more quickly than positive word of mouth.

The same applies to keeping customers happy. Research has shown that an unhappy customer talks to more people about their experience than a happy customer does, so you have to have systems in place for quickly placating anybody who is dissatisfied. If you fix their problem promptly and perhaps go beyond the call of duty in the process, they can be turned into evangelists rather than detractors.

" A word from the mouth is like a stone from a sling. SPANISH PROVERB

Increasing your visibility

One way to increase the visibility of your business is to get out into the community yourself. There's a good chance that your business, its products, its machinery or methods of production, or your own expertise could be of interest to the public. That gives you an opening to offer to speak to community groups, trade associations and schools. You could also volunteer to teach a course at a local school or college or adult education programme.

If you're not a confident public speaker, maybe someone else within the company can take this on. An outgoing, friendly, knowledgeable individual becomes a great ambassador for your business.

What are three groups or associations that might be interested in your product or service?

_____

_____

_____

If writing comes easier to you than speaking, you might be able to write a column for a local publication or a trade journal, or at least some one-off articles. These will all run with a short biography at the end, together with contact information or your website address. Later you can post copies on your website and use extracts if you publish an e-bulletin (more about these in Chapter Seven on new media).

What are three publications that might be interested in articles you or someone else in your business could write?

_____

_____

_____

These kinds of appearances and activities are not about making sales but about building up a reputation and public awareness. Obviously it makes most sense to target members (or perhaps future members) of your niche group, but sometimes simply raising your profile within your community pays in the longer run.

Time saver

If you write articles or a column, re-use the material on your website, in your newsletter and even as the basis of talks to community groups or schools.

Stay on top of what's being said about you

As well as promoting your own messages about your business, you need to stay aware of what others may be saying about you. Google offers you a free way to do this. Go to **http://www.google.com/alerts** and fill in your name, the name of your company, the name of your product or service and any other relevant terms. Select how often you want to be informed of any of these appearing in the media (once a week, once a day or as it happens) and enter your email address. You'll get a list of links to any mentions of the names or terms you have requested. This will enable you to stay on top of any positive or negative references and to take action accordingly. If it's praise, you may be able to turn this into a press release or other benefit; if it's something negative, you will be able to respond quickly to set the record straight.

Think of three or more keywords or phrases that apply to your business that you want to keep track of:

_____

_____

_____

Whatever media you use, knowing why people buy and how to tell your story to influence them is vital. Even if you decide to hire others to do this for you, it's good to understand the principles so that you can be sure they're doing a good job. In the next chapter, you'll find a quick course in persuasion and the essentials of effective copywriting.

Marketing power boost

Use the 1 + 1 = 3 method

To come up with clever ideas for events or activities that could make your product or service newsworthy, use the creativity technique I call '1 + 1 = 3'. It's simple but highly productive. You just combine two elements to see what this brings to mind. One of the elements will be your product or service. The other will be a randomly chosen word. Make a list of 20 or 30 such words before you start. They can be anything – an object, an emotion, a location, whatever. Here's a sample of six I picked randomly from today's newspaper:

→ hospital
→ zebra
→ debate
→ magazine
→ bank
→ anger.

By yourself or in a group, spend 20 minutes to see what new public relations or publicity ideas you can come up with when you put the two together. For example, let's say that your product is a powerful torch. Here are some top-of-the head ideas based on putting that together with the sample words above:

→ Hospital + torch = get statistics (or quote from an expert) on how many accidents at campsites or festivals are due to poor lighting. Write a press release offering tips on how to be safe if you're going to music festivals this summer. Of course, one of the tips would be to take along a powerful torch, but be sure to offer lots of other tips as well, so the whole thing doesn't look like just an advert.

→ Zebra + torch = link up with a zoo or association connected with protecting wild animals to produce a free booklet for children on how to observe wildlife in their back gardens or at nearby parks. Naturally a good torch always comes in handy, and if you're co-sponsoring the booklet, you certainly have the right to make one of the pages an advert for your product.

Now try this yourself, combining your product or service with one of the words in the list above, and jot down your ideas here:

_____

_____

_____

_____

Marketing power boost

Getting ready for your close-up

Does the idea of being interviewed on the radio make you nervous? It's a great tool for gaining credibility and exposure, so why not practise by calling some of the phone-in shows with your opinions on whatever they're talking about? Usually you'll give only your first name so nobody will know who you are, if you stumble or hem and haw the first few times it won't matter. Once you get used to talking on air you'll feel relaxed and be articulate. To prepare for television interviews, video yourself being grilled by colleagues. Ask them to be extra tough on you, so when you get into the real situation it will seem mild by comparison.

Web bonus

At our website, **www.forentrepreneursbooks.com**, click on the 'Marketing for Entrepreneurs' button. On the link for Chapter Five you'll find a video interview with PR expert Amanda Barry Hirst.

Key points

→ Branding means creating a strong association in the mind of the customer.

→ Two main ways of reaching customers is via advertising and public relations.

→ The main tool of public relations is the press release.

→ A press release should be concise, newsworthy and feature a strong headline.

→ To be a good guest on TV and radio, be able to talk in sound bites.

Next steps

What action will you take to apply the information in this chapter? By when will you do it?

_____

_____

_____

_____

Your marketing toolbox

Part Two

How to tell your story so they'll buy

Chapter Six

Marketing is about reaching people with your message, but if the message isn't powerful enough to motivate people to buy your product or service, it has been wasted. Jonathan Jay, the entrepreneur who made his fortune by establishing the first UK training academy for life coaches, told the *Sunday Times*: 'The most important thing is identifying the market you are selling to, but once you have found the market you have to craft the right message for it.'

This chapter provides a quick course in why people buy and how you can persuade them to understand the benefits of what you offer. This will include the basics of effective copywriting, using a formula that has long been known to Hollywood screenwriters but works equally well for marketing messages.

Why people buy

The foundation of all sales and marketing is awareness of one key fact: people buy based on emotion and then justify their purchase with logic.

It's easy to see that emotion rather than logic motivates people to buy Rolex watches, Rolls-Royce cars and Cristal champagne. But the rule doesn't apply just to luxury goods enjoyed by status seekers. Emotional appeals work with every type of product. The makers of dishwasher tablets assure you that you won't suffer the embarrassment of having spots on your drinking glasses when you throw a party. The producers of toothpaste tell you that your smile will be so sexy that members of the opposite sex will find you irresistible. The manufacturers of athletic footwear imply that when you wear their brand you'll be more like David Beckham or Michael Jordan.

Marketers have many ways to arouse the kinds of emotion that make us more likely to buy their products. The best book on this topic is *Influence: The Psychology of Persuasion*, by Robert Cialdini. For more detail and many entertaining case studies, I highly recommend reading Cialdini's book, but let's look at the key factors that he identified.

Reciprocation

We have been conditioned to believe that if someone gives us something, we should give them something, too. This concept explains the power of providing free samples. Not only does the customer have a chance to try out your product or service, but also it sets them up to be more inclined to do business with you afterwards. Maybe you have experienced this when you've tasted a food sample at a supermarket. Especially if the person handing out the samples has been friendly and pleasant, we are more likely to buy the product even if it wasn't all that great. It's not just true for little purchases either, it also plays a role when time-share salespeople lure you with a free lunch and some kind of small present. It's mostly the hard-sell pitch that does the work, but there is also an element of reciprocation at work. The same is true when someone offers you a free half-hour consultation.

This strategy does not have to be tricky in any way. Master vintner Manfred Esser calls his version of it 'guilt marketing', explaining, 'You treat your customers *so* well that you create a sense of obligation to come back to your product or service. And, even more than that, to become ambassadors for your company. They actually feel guilty if they forget about you.'

Commitment and consistency

When we have acted a certain way, from that point on we will feel internal pressure to be consistent and behave that way again. Charity solicitors ('charity muggers', shortened to 'chuggers') use this prin-ciple. They will begin by asking you whether you are aware of the destruction of the environment, or the hunger of African orphans, or the danger to highland gorillas. They will ask whether you oppose these things. Let's face it, none of us are going to say we're in favour of ecological disasters or hunger or poaching gorillas, so now you have established your commitment to their cause. What's the most consistent thing to do next? Donate some money, of course. This principle works just as well on paper as in person. The headline that reads, 'Do you finally want to lose weight and feel great?' makes most overweight people mentally say 'yes'. The commitment has been established and the reader is much more likely to sign up for the diet plan, the gym membership or the weight-loss supplement that is touted in the rest of the message.

Another manifestation of this principle is the up-sell. We agree to buy something and then the salesperson offers us a much better version of the product. We've already committed to buying the cheaper one, so getting us to move up to a more expensive but better version is easier than trying to get us to buy the more expensive one from a cold start.

Social proof

Remember when you told your mother or father you simply had to have some toy 'because all my friends have it?' Probably the answer was something like, 'If all your friends ran naked down the road, would you do it, too?' You may have said 'no', but actually, the best answer is, 'yes!' Social proof refers to the fact that we look to other people to see what is the right thing to do. Most people cannot stand being out of step with their peers.

A lot of people are especially eager to mimic the celebrities they admire. This accounts for the success of the blog, **www.celebrity-babies.com**. It shows what the babies of celebrities are wearing and gets an almost unbelievable 10 million page views a month. According to an article in the *Wall Street Journal*, in 2007 the site pulled in about £250,000 in advertising from companies including McDonald's and General Motors – companies eager to reach the young females who are the site's main visitors. The article quotes one mother who bought a £12 pack of camouflage-print socks for her son after seeing them worn by the son of rock singer Gwen Stefani. She said that now he has these socks, her son 'can be just as hot as any celebrity baby.' This may sound as sad to you as it does to me, but who are we to argue with £250,000 a year in income?

This principle also relates to the power of testimonials. If we see that someone we perceive to be like us or a celebrity we admire has endorsed a product or service, we are more likely to buy it. Strong testimonials from people willing to be identified by name and job position are great, but here are some other ways to use social proof:

→ Name companies using your product or service.

→ Say how many people have used your business or how many of your products have been sold.

→ Quote positive references to your business in the media.

→ Say how long you have been in business (assuming it's a long time).

→ Mention any awards your business has received.

→ If you have advertised on television or in any major magazines, include 'as seen on ITV' or 'in the *Guardian*' or 'as mentioned on Capital Radio'. Even though people know that you probably paid for such mentions, they still seem to have an effect.

All of these references reinforce the idea that your business is trusted by others and therefore can be trusted by prospective customers as well.

Social proof in the lemming household.

"And I suppose if all your friends wanted to jump off a cliff, you'd want to jump off, too!"

The likeability factor

There are two aspects of this principle. First, we are more likely to buy from someone we know and like; and second, we tend to like people we perceive to be most like ourselves. The similarity can be in appearance, manner of dress, age group, interests and so on. Slick salespeople take advantage of this by asking you about your interests and saying they share the same hobby. However, this principle can also be used honestly. The chances are that if you are selling tennis goods, for instance, you actually do have a major interest in tennis. Many entrepreneurs start their businesses out of frustration at not being able to find a way to fulfil a need they had themselves, so their shared interest with their customers is genuine. The marketing implications are that it is very useful to let your prospective customers get to know you a bit before you try to sell them anything and that it's important to stress what you have in common with them.

Another way to use this principle is to make sure that when you show the product or service being used, the people using it resemble your prospective customer. Customers respond not only to seeing people who resemble them as they are, but also to people who resemble how they'd like to be. Clothing catalogues usually use models who weigh a stone or two less than the typical customer. We like to imagine that we will look as good in these clothes as the models, and that prompts us to buy.

Marketing Hall of Shame

'Invented by a teacher...'

A key part of the story of Airborne, fizzy orange tablets that you dissolve in water and that supposedly kill germs and prevent colds, was that they were invented by a teacher who was frustrated at the number of colds suffered by her young students – and, therefore, herself. As well as promising a huge benefit, it took advantage of the likeability of that teacher, Victoria Knight-McDowell, and the appeal of the idea that an ordinary person had come up with something that all the scientific experts hadn't. The teacher was invited to appear on *The Oprah Winfrey Show*, and within a year the product's annual sales went from $21.4 million to more than $100 million.

It wasn't the story that came unstuck, but the claimed benefits. The Federal Trade Commission found that 'there is no credible evidence that Airborne products

… will reduce the severity or duration of colds, or provide any tangible benefit for people who are exposed to germs in crowded places.' In two settlements the company has set aside up to $30 million to pay consumers back for as many as six purchases. There is no contention that the product is unsafe or harmful and it continues to be sold, but with modified claims. Now the adverts say only that the vitamins and minerals in Airborne 'help support your immune system'.

It's a useful reminder to be sure that you can back up any claims you make about your product. Naturally, this is especially important for products in the medical and nutritional fields, but even outside those, making exaggerated claims is a quick way to lose credibility if suddenly someone disproves your assertions. No story will be strong enough to negate that damage.

Appeal to authority

We listen to authority figures because we assume they know more than we do about a particular subject. Politicians take advantage of this all the time, and a surprising number of people don't question what a prime minister or a president does because 'he must know more about it than we do'. Of course, that's probably true, but it doesn't mean that he's doing it for the greater good. Advertising uses this principle by getting authority figures like doctors to endorse products, or by referring to scientific studies that reveal the product is '10 per cent more effective' (usually without revealing what it's 10 per cent more effective than).

Sometimes it's enough to look the part. I have an acquaintance who got into the Academy Award ceremonies simply by dressing in a tuxedo and acting as though he belonged there. He ended up on stage at the end, singing 'There's No Business Like Show Business' with all the nominees that year.

The ethical use of this principle entails citing meaningful scientific studies or endorsements from authority figures who genuinely believe in the benefits of your product or service.

'A presumptuous little award...'

A prestigious magazine endorsing your product is a good example of the 'appeal to authority' principle. Therefore, when the restaurant Osteria L'Intrepdio, in Milan, was granted an Award of Excellence by *Wine Spectator* magazine, the owner must have been pleased. After all, *The Times* called the magazine 'the taste-maker for wine snobs around the world'. But the restaurant's 'owner', writer Robin Goldstein, wasn't bragging when this happened; he was chuckling – because the restaurant doesn't exist.

He had sent the magazine the restaurant's fake wine list, purposely loading it with wines that the magazine had given bad reviews, plus a cheque for $250 (£135). He set up a fake website with a few fake reviews and waited. Not too long afterwards, he received a plaque he could have hung on the restaurant's wall if it had had a wall, plus the right to list his establishment on the magazine's website. It turns out that the excellence award has generated more than $1 million for the magazine, and while they didn't do anything illegal, this has dented the credibility of their awards – and helped Mr Goldstein get publicity for his book, *The Wine Trials: 100 Everyday Wines Under $15 that Beat $50 to $150 Wines in Brown-Bag Blind Tastings*. So, from a marketing standpoint there was one winner and one loser.

From the nutritionist whose degrees turned out to be from a mail-order university to the author who hyped his own books on the Amazon website using false names, there is a long history of little scams designed to confer contrived status or praise upon a person or product. Sometimes the public are forgiving, sometimes not. It's better to stick to the truth.

Scarcity

Have you ever watched a group of children playing near a pile of toys? Little Jake is perfectly happy playing with his action figure and couldn't care less about the toy bus nearby – until little George grabs the toy bus. Suddenly Jake has to have the bus and screams blue murder if he doesn't get it away from George. Why? Because suddenly the bus is scarce. Maybe this goes back to our caveman times when most things were scarce, but it's a powerful factor. As evidence, consider how much money people pay for a postage stamp that has been mis-printed. There's no logical reason why a stamp missing a number or with the portrait of the Queen reversed should be more valuable than a normal one, but scarcity alone makes such stamps worth hundreds of thousands of pounds, if not more.

Marketers take advantage of this by creating limited editions of things they could actually produce in unlimited numbers, or they make a particular item available for only a limited time. It's also a powerful factor at auctions, where we not only want to get the unique item that's up for sale, but also want to make sure nobody else gets it. We may be older but we're not so different from little Jake and George. However, if a business says that something is in limited supply or available only for a short period and later we find out that the same product was withheld artificially, it can destroy trust. The iPhone provides a good example of real and fake scarcity. In the UK and the US there really was a huge demand on the first day the iPhone was released, and buyers camped outside Apple stores for hours (even days) ahead of time. In Poland buyers are more reluctant to pay the heavy monthly charges, so to drum up extra interest mobile operator Orange hired actors to create fake queues at 20 of their outlets.

Marketing Hall of Fame

Armstrong's yellow braclet

One of the most remarkable marketing phenomena of recent years was the incredible popularity of the 'Live Strong' yellow rubber bracelets sold in aid of the Lance Armstrong Foundation. 'Live Strong' is the cancer charity's motto, and yellow was the colour of Armstrong's jersey in the Tour de France. The wristbands were sponsored by Nike, who underwrote the production of the first 5 million. Sales really took off when Armstrong and his whole team wore them during the Tour de France for his sixth consecutive victory. Celebrities started wearing them, and suddenly they were a must-have item. When Oprah Winfrey challenged her television audience to break the record for how many were sold in one day, they bought more than 900,000 of them. To date more than 20 million have been sold.

What explains the success of this rather modest looking item which became a hot fashion accessory? Mostly the principle of social proof – the idea that if others, including celebrities, were supporting this cause, we should too, and as evidence of our commitment we could wear the highly noticeable wristband. Of course, its association with an athletic idol who overcame cancer was a strong factor, as was the timing, coinciding with his spectacular sixth victory. There was even a scarcity factor when there were not enough of the bracelets available to meet demand – counterfeiters got into the act at that point with bogus bands that, of course, didn't benefit the charity. But overall, it was a case of a combination of factors coming together at just the right moment and, in this case, the profits going to a worthy cause.

Tying your product to a charity can be a beneficial strategy, which works best when there is a logical connection between the product and the cause. A company that makes athletic shoes, for instance, might support a charity that helps build sports facilities for children in deprived areas, or an upmarket restaurant might donate 10 per cent of its profits for a month to an organisation that helps feed the poor.

Unless the product is one that brings in millions, it's a good idea to make sure that the percentage donated is substantial – saying 'we donate 1 per cent of our annual profits to end world hunger', for example, could make you seem miserly rather than generous. It may make more sense to donate 100 per cent of your profits for one day during a charity event, even if the sums would end up being the same.

Manipulation or human nature?

All of these techniques could be classed as manipulation, or simply as responding to human nature. My position is that if you are offering people something genuinely useful – not trying to cheat them or lie to them – then there's nothing wrong with using these methods of influence. In fact, not using them would put you at a serious disadvantage. Take a moment to think about how you can use them ethically in your own business by answering the questions below. Just jot down any ideas that occur to you; you'll have the chance to answer these again when you create your marketing master plan.

1 What is the main emotional appeal of your product or service?

_____

2 What useful thing could you give prospective customers to trigger the reciprocation effect?

_____

3 What could you get prospective customers to commit to that might lead to a later sale?

_____

4 Where can you get named testimonials from customers or clients that will act as social proof?

_____

5 What elements of your business will help customers to see the similarity between you and them – to take advantage of the likeability/similarity effect?

_____

_____

6 Who are the authorities your customers respect?

_____

7 How might you get those authorities to endorse your business?

_____

8 In what ways might you be able to use the scarcity effect genuinely?

_____

_____

_____

Since some customers (usually men) pride themselves on being immune to emotional appeals, it's wise also to give them the logical reasons for purchasing your product or service. They can then cite these reasons once their emotions have convinced them to buy.

The power of a story

Possibly the most effective marketing tool is to tell a story about your product or service, or about what the customers' lives will be like when they buy from you. Often these stories contain within them an appeal based on the motivators we have just covered.

In other words

A **story** is a sequence of events with a cause and effect connection. As novelist E.M. Forster noted, saying 'The king died and then the queen died' is merely a plot; saying 'The king died and then the queen died of a broken heart' is a story. It not only has a causal connection, but also an emotional element, which always makes a story stronger – and that's as true in marketing as in novels.

One example of a successful businessman who discovered the power of stories is Guy Watson, who left a top management job to set up as an organic farmer. He didn't like the cut-throat pricing of the wholesalers he was supplying, so he started delivering some boxes of his vegetables to households in the local area. He told *The Times*, 'The first boxes were a pretty crude offering, but when I met the customers it was immediately obvious that they were interested in where the food was from and what it tasted like. There was this pent-up demand for this connection with how the food was grown.' From that humble beginning, in which the story of

Marketing for Entrepreneurs

the local origins of the food was the catalyst, his company, Riverford, has grown in size and now employs 260 staff.

> **Story is far older than the art of science and psychology, and will always be the elder in the equation no matter how much time passes.**
>
> CLARISSA PINKOLA ESTES

Linking to existing stories

It helps if the story already exists and you just have to take advantage of it. Sometimes the story is the only thing that gives you the edge. For instance, the Cornish Sea Salt Company is harvesting salt from Cornwall's clear blue water and is finding there is considerable demand for it. The technology is not exclusive, so the same could be done on any coast, but entrepreneur Tony Fraser told the *Guardian*, 'The advantage we have is that people associate Cornwall with the cliffs, the beaches and the sea. So what better place to get your sea salt from?' In other words, his company has the advantage of a story that is already in people's heads.

A story about pens

One business that tells a story well is Turning Point (**www.turningpoint pens.com**). With the company's permission, I am reprinting here part of the story you will find on its website. As you read it, notice all the methods it employs:

> *The genesis of Turning Point started in 2000 when Matt Newton hand-turned his first writing instrument for his wife as a birthday gift. Under the tutelage of two master woodworkers, Matt was searching to find the place where his artistic skills would most impact the world. The moment the first writing instrument was finished by his hands, he knew he had found that place.*
>
> *He also realized that the vast majority of people were simply not aware of the amazing array and complexity of woods in the world.*

How to tell your story so they'll buy

There was also not one single pen company in the world who produced fine writing instruments solely out of fine woods. In 2001 Mr Newton started Turning Point with the vision of making the finest writing instruments period. Unbeknownst to Matt, he would end up being known for making pens with incredible historical significance.

In 2001 Turning Point produced 2 historic pens. The Jefferson Davis pen made from a 500 year old live oak from Mississippi where Jefferson Davis [president of the Confederate States of America during the American Civil War] read and spent his leisure hours under its massive branches. And the Union Station pen made from the 300 year old heart pine trusses of the Union Station shed in Nashville TN. A national landmark and engineering wonder.

... Four years and thousands of pens later Turning Point has been the leader in one-of-a-kind expedition for something different in a fine writing instrument. Isn't it time you had your Turning Point?

Let's look at what makes this a good story. First, there's a sympathetic protagonist – the first thing we are told about the man behind Turning Point is that he put a lot of effort into making a birthday present for his wife. Also, the fact that he wanted his artistic impulses to have an impact on the world is admirable. The story then arouses our curiosity by linking pens to wood and by referring to pens with 'incredible historic significance'. Then it gives examples of some interesting historic links that would be familiar to many Americans. It ends with a 'call to action' – the notion that it's time for you to be part of this story by buying a pen from this company.

Naturally, this story will have the strongest impact on two groups – pen lovers and history lovers. If you're both, as I am, the story becomes even more powerful. If you read this tale before you look at the pens sold on the site, their price (an average of about $200) doesn't seem so extreme any more. You're no longer comparing them to pens you might find at WH Smith for £10 or £20; the story has created a whole different context.

Even if your product or service is very different from pens, can you think of any way this story might serve as a model for you? If so, jot down your thoughts here:

Short stories work, too

Sometimes you can tell a story in one sentence. Dan Post of Duarte Design tells of a small health club that covered its windows in lists of the services available, such as 'customised meal planning systems', 'exercise programming', 'accountability and motivation', and 'psychological and emotional coaching'. There were very few customers. One day those signs disappeared and were replaced by a drawing of a deckchair with an abandoned set of clothes on it, and only three words: 'Look better naked'. Within weeks the place was buzzing with customers. Instead of listing features, the owner switched to one giant benefit, stated in a way that starts a story going in the head of the person who reads it.

Should you be part of the story?

With some brands the CEO becomes the public spokesperson for the business and the two become closely connected in the minds of the public. When we think of Virgin we think of Richard Branson. When we think of Apple we think of Steve Jobs. Having the CEO or another top executive be representative of the business helps to humanise it and can be a strong asset. The forms that this might take include appearing on TV or radio and in print ads, writing a company blog, having your photo on the website and in marketing materials, sending out email messages or e-bulletins signed by you, and being the one who talks to the media when they have questions.

However, there are also some dangers. For instance, rumours that Steve Jobs might be seriously ill (after overcoming some major health challenges a few years ago) created great anxiety among shareholders. When a company's image is so identified with one person, whatever happens to that person – whether it be illness, a legal problem or taking a strong political stance – impacts the business.

You also have to decide whether you have the right personality for being this much in the public eye. Some executives and entrepreneurs, like Branson, obviously thrive on it. Others prefer to be more private and stay behind the scenes. The decision is yours; the most important thing is to make the decision and stick to it.

Hollywood's storytelling secret you can use

For a long time Hollywood screenwriters have used a story structure that underpins many of the most successful films of all times. It's not so well known outside the film industry and remains a secret to most people writing marketing materials. If you use it you are almost certain to create a story that will grip your readers and keep them reading right through to the end – the part where you tell them what they need to do next, which is usually to buy your product or service.

This structure is often called 'the hero's journey', and it was first written about by the late mythologist Joseph Campbell in a fascinating book called *The Hero With a Thousand Faces*. This book caught the attention of a young film-maker named George Lucas. He went on to use this story structure as the basis for his *Star Wars* films and befriended the elderly Campbell. I have simplified the hero's journey into the following steps:

1 We meet the hero in his ordinary world. This is your customer or someone like them.

2 The call to action. Something happens in the hero's world to stir him out of his normal routine. It may be a problem or an opportunity.

3 The hero commits to a new path in order to solve the problem or take advantage of the opportunity.

4 He discovers allies and helpers, and perhaps a mentor, but also an enemy or opponent.

5 He encounters obstacles and overcomes them.

6 He experiences a moment of truth – a situation in which he will fail or succeed. Naturally, in marketing, he will always succeed, at least if he has taken advantage of your product or service.

7 He returns to his normal world, now richer in some way, and shares what he's learned or the treasure he's gained.

An everyday hero's story

Let's try this structure out on a very ordinary situation, stripped of any attempt to dress it up, just so you can see the bare bones of the story. Our hero in this case is Lucinda, a woman of generous proportions. She is going along in her ordinary life, but when she goes to have a check-up with her doctor, he tells her that her weight problem is now serious enough to be endangering her future health (the call to action).

She confides her problem to her best friend, who says she's joined a new gym that gives nutritional counselling as well as prescribing an exercise programme.

Lucinda enrols, too (committing to a new path).

At the gym she gets nutritional and exercise advice from experts (the helpers).

She exercises alongside her friend (an ally).

She's tempted to break her diet or skip her exercise session and some of her friends tell her not to bother dieting (the obstacles and the enemies).

She goes to a big party where all of her favourite tempting foods are practically calling her name (the moment of truth) – but she makes the right decision.

Some months later she goes back to see her doctor (her return to the normal world) and steps onto the scales. Hooray, she's lost two stone already and is on the way to her ideal, healthy weight.

At home, her husband and children comment favourably on how well she's done and are happy that she is no longer endangering her health and is preparing healthier food for them, too (sharing the treasure).

The story ends with details of how you, too, could have this happy ending if weight is an issue for you – and if it's not, you probably wouldn't have bothered reading it to the end.

Stripped to those essentials it may not sound very inspiring, but if it were told more colourfully, and especially if it were a true, first-person account, it could be a very strong story.

Your turn

Imagine you want to tell the story of someone who solves a problem or takes advantage of an opportunity by buying your product or service. To construct the skeleton of that tale, answer the following questions:

1 Who is the hero of this story (male or female – a typical customer)?

_____

2 What is the problem or opportunity and what makes them aware of it?

_____

3 What is the first step the hero would take?

_____

4 What kind of allies, helpers or mentors would the hero encounter? (This could be your product or service.)

_____

5 What kind of obstacles and enemies would the hero overcome with the help of your product or service?

_____

6 What would be the moment of truth, when the hero realises all the promised benefits of your product or service and finally overcomes the problem?

_____

7 How will things be better for the hero upon their return to the normal world?

_____

This is a good structure from which to construct a great case study or other marketing material. Now let's consider how you can make such material really come alive.

An even quicker way to shape the basic story of your business is to use a three-step fairy-tale construction: 'Once upon a time there was [describe your target customer]. One day, [describe the customer's problem]. Fortunately, there was a fairy godmother in the vicinity, named [your business], and she solved the problem by [describe how your business solves the customer's problem].' Now you have the core of your story and can expand it from there.

The two emotions that drive stories – and customers

There are two primal emotions behind most of what we do: hope and fear. In some stories, the hero goes forth on a valiant quest because he hopes to find the treasure – the golden apple, the princess's hand in marriage or the secret of eternal youth. In others, something invades his peaceful world and threatens him. Perhaps it's a dragon who steals his sweetheart or a wizard who places a curse on his family. He is scared but must overcome that fear in the course of his adventure.

If you doubt that hope still plays such a big part in our lives, just consider how many people buy a lottery ticket every week despite knowing that the odds against them winning are astronomical. Or look at Las Vegas, an entire city built on the hope of beating the odds that very clearly are against you.

Fear, of course, is equally rampant. Politicians use it to garner support and marketers use it to stir up our fear of getting old, or smelling bad, or not wearing the right thing and so on.

We'll take a closer look at the variety of uses of these emotions in a moment, but for now jot down three hopes that your product or service might tap into:

_____

_____

_____

Now jot down three **fears** that your product or service might help assuage:

_____

_____

_____

Make it emotional

The implication of the dominance of hope and fear is clear: when writing copy or telling your story, make it strong and make it emotional. The pen story starts with an emotional scene – someone making a present for his wife, hoping that she would be delighted by it. Even the one-liner that brought people to the gym, 'Look better naked!' appeals to our emotions – the fear that we'll look bad naked and the hope that if we look better naked maybe we'll get some action. One of the strongest emotions is lust, which is why so many adverts use sex as a lure, even when the product or service itself is far removed from matters of the flesh.

The pyramid of needs

In 1943 psychologist Abraham Maslow wrote about what he called the 'hierarchy of needs'. His theory was that there are five levels of human need that can be imagined as forming a pyramid. The most basic needs are at the bottom, and as each stage of needs is fulfilled, we move up to the next level in terms of what we desire. The levels, starting at the bottom, are:

→ physiological – food, water, breath, sleep, etc.;

→ safety – the need to feel secure in our existence;

→ love, affection, belonging – relationships with family, friends and our peer group;

→ esteem – valuing ourselves and being valued;

→ self-actualisation – doing what one was born to do, giving one's life a sense of meaning.

If we feel we are missing out on any of these levels, we are more inclined to act, either out of hope of getting more or fear of losing what we have. In our society most people have food, clothing and shelter but are anxious about the other levels. Let's take safety as an example. The headlines about terrorism have undermined that feeling. In response, most of us will 'buy' a political plan that tells us we'll be safer if we give up some liberties. We'll buy a personal alarm to carry around if we think it would scare away a mugger – especially if it is offered to us on a day that we've seen a headline about another stabbing on the streets.

At Maslow's next level, if someone can convince us that what they are selling will make us more loveable, we're very likely to buy if that's a realm in which we feel lacking. Even if we have a loving relationship, we may be motivated by the fear that we could lose the affection of someone who loves us if we don't look our best or smell our best, or if we don't buy them a diamond.

The power of hope and fear

There is nothing wrong with addressing people's fears if you have a product or service that will reduce their anxieties or offer them a solution to a problem that poses a genuine threat. Of course, a certain element of marketing and advertising is targeted to intensifying those fears in order to sell products, and that's where you have to refer to your own sense of morality to decide where to draw the line.

Hope ties in to Maslow's hierarchy in the same way. For each of the levels people have dreams of how they would like their life to be. They have an image of the beautiful home in which they would like to live; they want their children to grow up in attractive, green, safe neighbourhoods; they would like to have many friends and a loving relationship with their families. At the level of self-actualisation, perhaps they hope to express themselves by writing or painting or making music. All of these aspirations have an emotional connection that you can draw upon in your marketing stories as well. If you can show people how your product or service can help them to achieve their dreams, they will beat a path to your door.

How to make your words come alive

You should now have a pretty good idea of the story you can tell, the emotions that underpin that story and the structure of the story. The next challenge is using language to achieve the desired impact. Your first tool is our old friend, the sound bite. Just to remind you, a sound bite is a pithy, quotable statement. Many people don't realise that it's much harder to say less than to say more. A quote that has been attributed to Mark Twain, Rudyard Kipling and others is a postscript to a lengthy letter: 'I'm sorry this is such a long letter, I didn't have time to write a shorter one.'

From sound bites to story

To give you a practical example of how a series of sound bites can make a story come alive, let me share a personal story. Recently a journalist from the *Independent on Sunday* rang me to say she wanted to write an article about my book, *Focus: The Power of Targeted Thinking*, and especially on why we all procrastinate. In the book I have the luxury of devoting an entire chapter to this topic; in the interview I'll have a few minutes at best, out of which she will pick maybe half a dozen sentences to quote directly. So my first job is to capture her attention right away with the big idea behind the story.

My sound bite summary is that **procrastination is the result of a battle going on in our brains.**

Good sound bites make the other person want to know more, and I assume that this statement will make her ask, 'How so?' That gives me the opening to explain that **the logical left brain says, 'I should do THAT'. The emotional right brain says, 'But I want to do THIS.'**

This statement sets up a conflict, and we always want to know how a conflict turns out, so I can add, **when logic fights emotion, usually emotion wins**. With procrastination, **sometimes neither one wins** – it's a draw, and you end up doing neither this nor that. **You have none of the fun and all of the guilt.**

All of the bold-faced phrases are the sound bites. When you put them together, they tell the story. I was a journalist for a number of years, so I know from experience those are the kind of phrases reporters listen for and that will end up in the story. They can even be used as pull quotes – those snippets that are taken out and featured in larger type to attract someone to read the whole article.

In the interview I will go on to describe my solution to this problem in similar terms, again trying to include a sound bite now and then and sticking to ideas and images that are easy to relate to. People can understand the idea of a war between logic and emotion because it's vivid and they have experienced that embattled feeling themselves. And the phrase 'none of the fun and all of the guilt' is a concise description of that state we've all been in when we end up doing neither what we should nor what we want.

Your turn

Can you imagine how the strategy of using such statements also helps you in writing adverts, sales copy and the other kinds of marketing material? Have a go yourself by answering these questions as though you were being interviewed, and try to come up with some sound bites as you go along.

1   How would you describe the problem that your product or service solves? (Hint: what is it like? What's a good metaphor?)

_____

_____

2   How would you describe your solution? (Again, can you come up with a metaphor that evokes an image?)

_____

_____

3   What's the best thing about your product or service?

_____

_____

Write with the power of NLP

The other writing strategy that will ensure that your marketing materials really connect with your target audience is based on Neuro Linguistic Programming (NLP; you may remember that this was the origin of the 'three positions' exercise in Chapter Four). One of the basic tenets of NLP is that individuals have their own way of encoding their experience, using a combination of their visual, auditory, kinaesthetic, gustatory and olfactory representational systems. In other words, we experience things through sight, sound, touch (and feelings), taste and smell, but most people favour one or more of those over the others.

Often, people unwittingly reveal which system they depend on the most by the terminology they use. For example, one person might say, 'Yes, I *see* what you mean'; another might say, 'I *hear* what you're saying'; and others might say, 'I have a good *feeling* about that', 'That sounds like a *sweet* deal,' or, 'I think that idea *stinks!*'

NLP suggests that one way to establish rapport with a person is to work out what their primary representation system is, and then use language that matches that system. Naturally, when we are writing we can't know which system a reader prefers, so our strategy has to be to use most, if not all, in our marketing materials, preferably quickly in order to hook the reader.

For example, let's say that your product has a USP connected to giving great customer service. You might want to contrast that with the poor standard of such service provided by others in your industry. In a brochure or on your website, you could feature a chart that represents people's level of unhappiness with typical customer service (visual), a transcription of some of these complaints or, on the website, a recording of them (auditory); you might also write or say that 'we have a feeling that this is the number one problem customers like you face at the moment' (kinaesthetic). You might even say that the current level of customer service at most companies leaves a bad taste in customers' mouths (gustatory).

Similarly, when thinking about how to convey all the benefits of your product, it can be useful first to imagine what your customers will *see* when they receive the benefits of your product or service, what they will *hear*, what they will *feel* and (if appropriate) what they will *taste* and *smell*.

If you outsource the creation of your marketing materials, you can check whether the people doing it for you have used this potent method and the other techniques revealed in this chapter. If you are creating the materials yourself, don't worry if your first draft isn't as good as it could be. Somebody observed that 'all writing is rewriting'. Just get down a rough draft of your marketing messages quickly, knowing that you can always go back and improve them.

The secret of effective critiquing

Critiquing our own material is difficult. One of the reasons is that typically we try to evaluate our work when we are in the wrong state. The creative state, in which we come up with ideas and write them down, is different from the critical state, in which we judge material against certain criteria. Trying to be critical when we're still in the creative state doesn't work very well.

The solution is to change your state when you are evaluating what you've written. Don't evaluate in the same location as you create. If you create at your computer, take the material to the living room or the kitchen, or to a coffee shop. If you listen to one kind of music when you write, don't listen to it when you evaluate. To get further distance from the material, print it out in a different typeface from the one in which you composed it. As you read through, pretend that someone else wrote it and you've been hired as a consultant to suggest ways to fix the weak spots. All of these methods enable you to see what you've written with fresh eyes. Once you've noted what changes are required, go back into your creative state and make the changes. You can alternate between these two states several times until you're sure the material is really good. It may help you to review the key points in this chapter between drafts.

> ### Toolkit
>
> For more information on how to write powerfully, see my book, *Your Writing Coach*, published by Nicholas Brealey Publishing. It takes you all the way from initial idea through to publication. You'll also find helpful information on the associated website, **www.yourwritingcoach.com**.

Marketing power boost

Universal emotions

How many basic story plots are there? There are all kinds of theories, but the one thing people agree upon is that there are certain key emotions that are universal and that underpin the stories we tell. Knowing what these are can make it easier for you to construct a story of your business that will resonate with your potential customers. In their book *Steal This Plot*, June and William Noble write about these emotions as being crucial:

→ vengeance

→ catastrophe

→ love and hate

→ grief and loss

→ rebellion

→ betrayal

→ persecution

→ self-sacrifice

→ survival

→ rivalry

→ discovery (quest)

→ ambition.

Any of these could be a key element of telling the story of how your business got started or how your product or service can impact the lives of your customers. For instance, maybe what you offer can help people cope with some catastrophe or be more likely to win the love of someone in their life, or can help them feel like rebels or further their ambitions. By yourself or in a group with some of your colleagues, go through this list and identify which ones will help you tell the story of your business in the most dramatic and appealing way. Jot down your thoughts below or on a separate sheet:

_____

_____

_____

_____

_____

_____

Web bonus

At our website, **www.forentrepreneursbooks.com**, click on the 'Marketing for Entrepreneurs' button. On the link for Chapter Six you'll find an audio track that reveals several other useful story structures you can use in your marketing, including the 'sand in the face' storyline.

Key points

→ People buy based on emotion and justify their purchase with logic.

→ The emotional triggers that prompt people to buy include:

— reciprocation;
— commitment and consistency;
— social proof;
— likeability;
— appeal to authority;
— scarcity.

→ Stories are powerful marketing tools.

→ You can make yourself part of your brand's story.

→ One of the most powerful story structures is the 'hero's journey'.

→ Hope and fear are the two emotions that drive stories – and customers.

→ Colourful, sensory-based language and specific details make a story come alive.

Next steps

What action will you take to apply the information in this chapter? By when will you do it?

_____

_____

_____

_____

New media, new opportunities (if you know how)

Chapter Seven

The new media offer you plentiful opportunities to expose people to your product or services in many different ways. You may be selling directly from your website, keeping subscribers posted on new developments with an e-bulletin or creating a blog, or vlog (video blog), or podcast to connect even more with your customers. And, of course, you may also have a presence on the social networking sites, such as Facebook and MySpace.

It's about trust

Especially with the social networking sites, some people don't get it. They say that if they can't use it to actually sell, what's the point? The biggest benefits of many types of new media are establishing yourself as a trustworthy expert in your field and establishing relationships with potential customers or clients. The more you become someone people know, like and trust, the more likely it is that they will buy from you. Therefore, the point of a Facebook page for you and your business isn't primarily to sell your product or service directly – it's to 'sell' yourself.

Avoid the temptation to use any of these media just because you can. If you want to have a private blog or podcast for the fun of it, that's great. But on the business level, any method you use to communicate with customers must serve a particular purpose. When you know exactly who you want to reach and why, it becomes much easier to decide which mechanism to use.

Publishing an e-bulletin

One marketing tool that is actually appreciated by potential customers – if it's done right – is the periodic e-bulletin (which may also be called an e-newsletter or an ezine, pronounced 'e-zeen'). Of course, it has to be useful to the recipient. Once again, we're back on the subject of benefits and 'what's in it for me?' If you're sending this e-bulletin to your niche, you already know what interests them, and that makes it easy to work out what your content should be. It should educate or entertain, ideally both. As UK marketing expert Nigel Temple points out, 'Increasingly, we will see promotional campaigns which are primarily educational in nature and which offer useful, relevant, interesting and informative help and advice. This approach is especially relevant for businesses on limited budgets.'

This e-bulletin need not be long; in fact, given how much time pressure your customers are under these days, it's best to limit it to one or two pages. Naturally you don't want to risk having it mistaken for spam, so you will have to ask people to opt in to the mailing list and to confirm that request.

Attracting e-bulletin readers

The challenge is getting people to subscribe. You should mention the e-bulletin, and how to request it, on your business cards, on your printed brochures, prominently on your website and even on invoices. If you give speeches you can hand out sign-up sheets, and if you have a retail outlet you can also give customers a sign-up card along with their receipts.

One way to motivate sign-ups is to offer a useful report or other incentive free of charge. A survey by interactive and email marketing agency eROI revealed that the most popular incentives and the percentages of users of each are:

→ a newsletter subscription (88 per cent);

→ access to exclusive content (29 per cent);

→ discounts or coupons (24 per cent);

→ contests (22 per cent).

Once you have some subscribers, ask them to let their friends know about the e-bulletin and consider offering an additional incentive for anyone who sends you three names and email addresses to whom you can send a sample. Naturally, you should not sign up these people; just send them one sample and ask them whether they wish to subscribe.

Put it on autopilot

There are any number of automated systems that will handle the mailings for you. You can use your search engine to look for 'ezine mailing services'. Some of the services charge by the number of subscribers and offer unlimited mailings, while others charge by the number of messages you send per month, so it's best to compare and select the one that best fits your needs. Two that have been around for some time and are highly regarded are constantcontact.com and aweber.com. I've used the latter to collect names and automatically send them an eight-part mini-course (the incentive), one part per week.

The frequency with which you send out the e-bulletin is up to you, but monthly generally is good. It's best if you send it out at roughly the same time every month so that customers expect it. You can actually write it whenever you want, and then cue the system to send it out on a certain date.

Usually you will be offered the choice of sending out the e-bulletin in HTML, which allows you to use graphics and different fonts, or text only, which looks plain but is readable by all recipients. Most services will allow your subscribers to choose which one they want when they sign up. They will also offer readers a way to unsubscribe instantly if they are no longer interested.

What to write

What should be the content of your e-bulletin? Generally, it should be anything that you feel would interest your target group. This includes the following, always being sure that any item relates specifically to the topic at hand:

→ Tips and techniques for being more effective or to save time.
→ Ways to save money.
→ New ways to use your product or service.
→ Case studies of how your product or service has solved someone's problems. Keep it factual rather than just a glorified advertisement.

- → Interviews with experts.
- → Frequently asked questions about your area of expertise.
- → Summaries of important developments.
- → Brief book reports.
- → An 'agony aunt or uncle' column, in which you answer emails or letters sent to you.
- → Offbeat facts or stories.
- → Reports from conventions, workshops or other events you have attended.
- → Links to relevant videos on YouTube or other sites.
- → Buyers' guides.
- → Opinion pieces based on your expertise.

Naturally, you can provide a mix of types of content and you will want to include information about your company or your newest product or service. If 80 per cent of the content is useful, subscribers will happily accept the 20 per cent that is a sales message. This can take the form of a banner advert or brief text with links through to your website or a sales page.

In addition to good content, the e-bulletin should have a personality. We all are exposed to so much bland verbiage that we really enjoy encountering something that stands out. You may risk alienating a few people, but remember the dictum that the person who tries to please everybody ends up pleasing nobody.

If your e-bulletin is longer than a page or two, it's a good idea to list the stories or features at the top and number them, so that readers can skip to the ones they want to read. You can also make this list clickable so that they are taken right to the feature they select. Most of the time you will want to keep the articles short, but if you do feature a longer article, start with an executive summary – a couple of sentences that explain the basic message.

A typical e-bulletin

If you'd like to see a sample e-bulletin, you can sign up for my free monthly creativity and productivity e-bulletin, *Brainstorm*, by sending an email request to **BstormUK@aol.com**. As you'll see, every edition features five brief articles, each with a suggested action step, and an inspirational quote. Sometimes I include a '60-Second Book Review', which relates the key points of a new book on creativity or productivity. I also include a paragraph of information about my latest book, workshops I'm offering or special offers on the information products I sell. I always set that apart from the rest of the text in some way, so that people will not think I'm trying to sneak in an advert disguised as a news or instructional item. I like to keep the sales aspect quite low key, but many e-bulletins feature several adverts and sometimes Google AdWords or other revenue-producing links. Generally I send out the e-bulletin the second week of each month. At the time of writing, this e-bulletin has about 3,000 subscribers.

Marketing Hall of Fame

'Fnac learns by doing'

French retailer Fnac started an e-commerce division in 1999 and decided to build a relationship with its customers via an electronic newsletter. This was especially important because the online site was not allowed to undercut the prices in the Fnac stores. The newsletter went out once a week to more than 1 million people. However, the system's shortcomings soon became obvious: it was unable to report how many of these people actually opened the newsletter or how many unsubscribed at any given point, and there was no link to the inventory online or in the stores. Furthermore, the mailings had to be done by IT specialists and the same newsletter went out to everybody; there was no way to individualise mailings based on what customers had bought or searched for.

In 2004, Fnac totally revamped the system. Now it's run by marketing people, not the IT department, and it can give immediate feedback on whether any item is in stock. The system saves information about the preferences of every customer and what they've searched for on the site, and it uses that to send out a variety of newsletters, each with different offers. That information also triggers notices about book signings, concerts hosted in the stores and other events of interest. According to *electronicRetailer* magazine, the newsletter has an opening rate of 20 per cent, which is excellent for this type of message, and the newsletter drives 10 per cent of the site's traffic. Fnac sends out some 40 million emails a month, with between 10 and 25 per cent of total sales coming from buyers responding to a mailing. Fnac is the number-one retail site in France – in no small measure due to the fact that where the use of e-bulletins and email is concerned, it learned from its mistakes.

Make targeting easy

Even if you start with an e-bulletin or email marketing campaign that goes to all your customers, make sure that the system you are using allows you to segment your customers in order to target subsets of that population. A service like aweber.com is set up to make that relatively easy, and you don't have to be an IT genius to use it. The more information you are able to gather about your customers – ethically, of course, and with their permission – the more specifically you can meet their needs. It will also allow you to determine which segments are most responsive to which kinds of marketing effort. You may find, for instance, that one part of your target population loves to get lots of emails, while another gets annoyed (and unsubscribes) if they feel you are bombarding them with too much information.

The mailing services will show you how many people opened the e-bulletin. Don't be shocked when you see that your opening rate is not 100 per cent. If it's 60 per cent you are doing well; between 20 per cent and 30 per cent is more typical. This doesn't mean that subscribers don't value the e-bulletin, but sometimes they may be especially busy and zap a whole bunch of emails at one time. If you ever feel you're carrying too much dead wood, you can request that people confirm that they want to continue to receive the publication. However, since your only cost is the fee for the mailing service, carrying people who open the e-bulletin only once in a while costs you almost nothing – and you never know when one of them may turn into a customer.

Is an e-bulletin right for you?

To help you decide whether producing an e-bulletin is right for your business, jot down your answers to the following questions:

1 What kind of information or entertainment that is relevant to your business would your customers value?

_____

_____

_____

2 What kind of personality would be most appropriate for an e-bulletin for your business? (Examples: authoritative, informal, gossipy, humorous.)

_____

3 How often do you think you'd be prepared to send out an e-bulletin? (Choose between weekly, every two weeks or monthly.)

_____

4 Who in your business would be most qualified and capable of writing your e-bulletin? Or would you want to outsource it?

_____

One good way to find out whether e-bulletins are right for you is to create a dummy or prototype. Run it by some of your current customers or members of your niche and get their reactions. Ask them to give you honest feedback about the content, the presentation and the proposed frequency. You can create several different versions and check which one your customers find the most useful and appealing.

Do you blog?

As you probably know, a blog is an online site in diary form. The most typical format features items that are added periodically – anything from several per day to once in a while. The newest item, or post, appears above the previous one.

Additionally, there can be pages that don't change – for instance 'about' pages that give information regarding the person or company behind the blog. It can also include links to other blogs or websites, a calendar of events, adverts, and many other features. In fact, blogs are now so versatile that they are beginning to take the place of websites, mostly because it's so much easier to create and update a blog. One example of a blog used in this way is **www.focusquick.com** – the site that accompanies my book, *Focus: The Power of Targeted Thinking*. This includes video interviews, audio features, articles and much more.

Keep it relevant

It's true that there are millions of personal blogs, on which we can follow young Alfie's progress through his piano lessons or find out whether Fluffy has recovered yet from that fungus that was making her fur fall out, but there are also many business-oriented blogs that provide substantial benefits to their creators. It takes some work to keep up a blog, especially once you commit yourself to posting new items at a regular rate. However, it can be worthwhile in terms of public relations and even for generating new business. The blog becomes one of the public faces of your business, and those who subscribe to it will have regular exposure to your ideas, your products and your personality (just as with e-bulletins, blogs with personality are more effective). Robert Jenson, CEO of the Jenson Group, told *Business 2.0*, 'Rather than blogging stream-of-consciousness opinions or using the venue as a diary of sorts, I educate visitors on important, universal industry matters. I try my utmost to ensure that the content I post is not just applicable and of interest to those in Las Vegas, where I operate, but also to any real estate consumer nationwide.'

The functions of a blog

A blog can:

→ keep customers up to date with your latest offerings;

→ help to establish a dialogue with customers, if you choose to allow visitors to leave comments in response to posts;

→ give you an outlet for responding quickly to any developments in your field or your company;

→ raise your profile as an expert or authority in your field;

→ give you an additional advertising outlet via adverts on the site;

→ list other sites with whom you establish link exchanges (in other words, you link to their site and they link to yours, thereby giving both additional exposure);

→ bring in revenue if you allow Google AdWords or another company's adverts to appear on it – naturally, this will be interesting to potential advertisers only once you are drawing a substantial number of visitors.

It is only the shallow who do not judge by appearances. OSCAR WILDE

Looks are important

A blog looks more appealing when you add some visual interest as well. A blog can easily show still photos or embed videos as well as audio files. On my writing blog I use a different small image for each of my posts. You can see it at **www.timetowrite.blogs.com**. I source the images from **www.clipart.com**. There is a very reasonable fee for a year's subscription, which gives you a choice of 10 million downloadable illustrations and photos. They are sufficiently high resolution to look fine on a blog or website, and if you want higher resolutions versions to use with print materials you can buy them for an additional fee.

Time saver

To save time, write a group of posts at one time, gather all the visuals at once and resize them all for the web, if necessary. You can then put all the posts on your blog to be issued once a day or whatever frequency you've decided upon.

Marketing for Entrepreneurs

Where to host?

You have a lot of options for hosting your blog. I use Typepad for the blog mentioned above (hosting information at **www.typepad.com**). For a small monthly fee it hosts my blog with no adverts – some free hosting companies place adverts on your blog. The other most popular option is WordPress (**www.wordpress.com**), where you can have your blog hosted free of charge, or pay a small monthly fee for a more sophisticated version that you host on your own server (**www.wordpress.org**). Many web servers now make it very easy for you to host a WordPress or other blog on your own site. This is preferable because it gives you the security of knowing that all your material remains totally under your control. This own-hosted version is a bit more complicated to set up, but WordPress offers free tutorials on its site that the average non-techie can understand, or you could hire someone to do it for you relatively inexpensively.

Danger!

Although it's unlikely to happen, if you're hosting your blog on someone else's site and that site goes out of business, all of your material could be lost. Back up all of your blog content periodically just in case.

A blog case study

One entrepreneur who has benefited from adding a blog to his site is Joey Shamah, whose company, Eyes, Lips, Face Cosmetics, sells a variety of beauty products. He told *Entrepreneur* magazine that when he added a gossipy blog and advice column and some other interactive features, his sales doubled and the average length of time a visitor spends on the site increased from 4 minutes to 13 minutes.

Attracting blog readers

As with websites, putting up a blog and keeping it current is only half the battle. It's all a waste of time if nobody bothers to read it. So how do you attract readers? As with an e-bulletin make sure that all your materials, including the signature line of your emails, mention your blog address. When I send out my e-bulletin, I always include a postscript that says, 'If you haven't looked at my blog lately, you've missed posts on…' and then I describe the posts I think sound most interesting. It always causes a spike in page views.

Allowing people to leave comments on your posts makes it an interactive experience and helps build traffic. You can opt to keep comments hidden until you have checked them to make sure they are not spam or obscene, or otherwise objectionable. When the company, Honest Tea, which had a USP based on being natural, announced that Coca-Cola would acquire 40 per cent interest in the brand, customers went to the company's blog to complain. Chief executive Seth Goldman told the *Washington Post*: 'We gave a very loud voice to the people who said they weren't happy with this decision.' He used the blog to answer the criticisms. He didn't win over everyone, but he notes: 'The blog at least helps people see how we think about it.'

Marketing Hall of Shame

'Cowgate'

Back in 2003, Dr Pepper/7Up launched a flavoured milk product called Raging Cow. Flavours included Berry Mixed Up, Chocolate Insanity and Jamocha Frenzy. To make their young target audience aware of Raging Cow, the company, in conjunction with marketing agency Richard Interactive, recruited ten teens to promote it in otherwise authentic blogs. Apparently the teens were told not to mention their connection with the company but it leaked out, to the annoyance of the blogging community, which saw this means of communication being corrupted by hidden advertising. The company's rejoinder was that the teenagers were not paid and were free to say anything they wanted about the product, even that they hated it. However, when you consider that the youngsters were flown to Dallas, Texas, to try the drink and were given drink samples and promotional products, it's easy to predict that they'd probably not say they hated it. One of them admitted that she was hoping for a job with the advertising agency. Other bloggers organised a boycott of Raging Cow which received a lot of press attention. The drink seems to have disappeared since.

Although there are still companies that give free samples of their wares for review and some agencies that pay bloggers to mention certain products, in general the blogosphere is in agreement that such arrangements should be out in the open.

Blog with care

There is one major warning about blogging: whatever you put on a blog is public. Very public. With an e-bulletin you would probably look over the material to make sure it's correct and appropriate; with a blog it's all too easy to dash off a post that seems fine at the time and then realise, only after you have received angry comments or even press attention, that in the heat of the moment you included something that was intemperate, libellous, confidential or otherwise inappropriate. Therefore, it's always a good idea to get someone else in your company to look over your post before you make it public. If you do make a mistake, correct it as soon as possible and apologise, if that's required – but whatever you do, don't try to cover it up or deny you ever wrote it. You can go back and edit a post, but someone somewhere probably has a copy of the original.

Your blogging policy

Another issue is your company policy regarding blogging on the part of your employees. Naturally employees have the right to blog about their own lives and opinions, but if they are in a position in which they represent the company it's not difficult to cross the line. There have been several high-profile cases of bloggers being fired for this. The best policy is to discuss the matter with your employees before there is a problem. Be clear that making negative comments about the company or their job, or revealing commercially confidential information, is not acceptable, but also offer to discuss any questions they have on a one-to-one basis.

Not every company will want a blog. Walter J. Carl, professor of communications at Northeastern University in Boston, Massachusetts, has studied blogging and points out that it's important to make sure that the blog fits within the existing culture of the company. If a company leans towards being secretive, a blog is not the right marketing tool.

Are you podcasting or vlogging?

A podcast is like a radio show on the internet but instead of being on the air at a particular time it can be listened to or downloaded at anytime. A vlog (or video blog) is the video version. They can cover any subject, be any length, have any number of participants and be produced at any interval you like.

In other words

Blogs are websites in which entries appear in order. They can contain text, videos and audio, as well as permanent pages and links. **Podcasts** are a series of audio recordings that can be listened to on the internet or downloaded. **Vlogs** (also called video blogs) are like podcasts, but in video format.

A podcast's defining characteristic is that it is an audio file. Some of the advantages of podcasts, compared to blogs or text on a website, are as follows:

→ They can be listened to on an iPod or other MP3 player, as well as via computers. This makes them appealing to people who want to have something to listen to while commuting or exercising.

→ For certain kinds of material such as interviews, an audio version gives a lot more atmosphere and a sense of the people who are expressing themselves. It tends to create a more intimate bond with the listener than text does with a reader.

→ Some people feel more comfortable talking than writing, so they find podcasts easier to create.

→ It's easy to mix a variety of elements, such as commentary, music, interviews, jingles, etc. – in other words, anything that you've heard on the radio can also be done on a podcast.

However, podcasts can also have some disadvantages, including the following:

→ People may pay less attention when listening, especially if they are doing something else at the same time, such as driving.

→ If the listener misses something, it's harder to go back and repeat than it is simply to look at a previous sentence in a text format.

→ Some people hate the sound of their own voice and prefer to write.

→ Podcasts require more work to put together, including audio editing, finding and adding copyright-free music, etc. Naturally, the more complex the format, the more technical work required.

→ At this point, people are more used to accessing and reading blogs than listening to podcasts, although that is gradually changing.

"Yes, dear, I know you have a podcast, but that doesn't mean you should change your name to M C Forty Pence Hammer!"

The video option

Vlogs are similar to podcasts and can be downloaded to video iPods and other players, as well as hosted on your own site. Of course, they require people to look at them as well as listen, so they're not good for anybody who is driving or working out at the gym. When deciding between a podcast and a vlog, the obvious question is whether there is an important visual component to the information you want to impart. If it's mostly going to be a talking head, you might as well stick with audio only.

As with blogs, the frequency with which you produce new episodes is not as important as being consistent, so that listeners will come to expect something from you every week or every month.

Before you commit...

The biggest questions for you are whether or not your business lends itself to a blog, vlog or podcast, and whether it's something you are interested in doing and have the time to commit to or the funds to outsource. They can be especially appropriate for businesses that are in a position to generate a lot of useful content, such as the latest developments in your field, 'how to' programmes related to your products or interviews with key people of interest to your target population. Those kinds of feature will draw readers, listeners or viewers because it is clear what's in it for them. It must also be equally clear what's in it for you and whether the payoff in terms of new leads or recognition for your business or for you as an expert is worth the effort.

Hardware and software

If you decide to create a podcast, one of the easiest ways to do this is to use the GarageBand software that is part of the inexpensive iLife suite of programmes for the Mac. It offers a specific option for recording and editing podcasts. For PC users the free Audacity software is a good choice. You can use various kinds of microphone, but the one I highly recommend is the Snowball USB microphone that plugs right

Marketing for Entrepreneurs

into your computer. If you are doing on-location interviews, one of the best portable recorders is the Edirol R-09.

If you're producing a vlog, you will need a reliable video camera, but it doesn't need to be an expensive one if you are going to distribute the material only on the internet. You can use the video function of your digital camera or one of the inexpensive and simple video recorders, like the Flip, for brief interviews and for grabbing informal footage. The biggest drawback of these is that they don't have inputs for an external microphone, so if your sound source is more than a foot or two away the audio can be weak. Also, generally, they have no zoom, or a very limited zoom, so the only way to get a closer shot is to move in. But there are now some great video cameras, especially from JVC, Sony and Canon, that will accommodate an external microphone and even give you high-definition images (not that you need them for the internet) for less than £400.

In most cases, Apple's iMovie, a part of the very inexpensive iLife suite of software programmes, is sufficient for editing. At the time of writing, iMovie 6 is still available via download and I find it preferable to the dumbed-down later version. There are similar inexpensive options for the PC user.

Expert interview
Richard Tierney on creating online video

The following interview with Richard Tierney gives you some specifics on how to create video for online use. Richard's company, Reachout Productions, has created videos for BMW, Channel Four, Zurich Finance, Ecclesiastical, HP:ICM, Barclays and KPMG, among many others.

Richard, putting video on the internet seems to be the hot thing at the moment.
Video on the internet isn't new – it's just now that some tipping point has been reached with broadband access so most folk can actually watch videos online. Most importantly, this means that the commissioners of these videos are also now in the habit of watching video online, so they understand when a creative agency suggests it. We video folk have been plugging away at this for ages, but now there is almost no resistance to the idea.

A lot of people hope to create a video that goes viral. Any observations about that?

My personal view (and it's only that) is that the more personal a message, the more viral it goes. No one forwards a corporate video unless it's for all the wrong reasons … and I have huge numbers of those. … So a personal viewpoint and humour are the things that get sent along. If you think about it, that's the same as forwarding text emails – it's got to be relevant or funny and preferably both.

I'd like to mention one important point. When non-professionals make films for their own use, to send to friends or to show at a business meeting, they can pretty much get away with ignoring copyright. If infringements are made it is incredibly unlikely to come to the attention of the copyright holder and even less likely that action will be taken. However, if short films are uploaded to company websites then for copyright purposes they can be deemed to have global distribution. That's what the internet is for after all. So if your viral campaign is a success then you will get a lot of attention from corporate lawyers who want to find any reason to share in your success. For this reason original music, images and performances are essential if you want to keep the profits of your endeavours.

Although we don't necessarily expect these kinds of video to match the production quality of a BBC show, what are the most important things to keep in mind from a production standpoint?

There is a perception that 'quality isn't important' but actually the truth is that 'quality needs to be appropriate', so if your script is knockout, then perhaps the framing, camerawork and lighting don't need to be so good. If it's a visual gag then the pictures are much more important. The fact is, using very cheap equipment you can get great results but you need to think carefully about each aspect. It's not difficult to find out about three point lighting, crossing the line, decent set up and punch lines, close mic'ed audio and so on, but you do need to think about all these things carefully and not assume that you are able to do them.

The main difference I see between the professional crews I work with and budding amateurs or students is that the professionals have solved all those many problems years ago and now don't have to think about the technique – they just get on with the content and telling the story in the best way they know how. If you've not done this before you need to take the time to think and learn about *everything*.

We know that the cost of video equipment has come down, but can you give a rough estimate of what someone would have to spend in order to create acceptable videos, with decent sound and lighting equipment included?
First, if this is your first attempt: don't buy – rent! Do this a few times until you find out what is important for you. I regularly work with about ten cameramen, and apart from a camera and tripod they all have different sets of equipment depending on the type of work they do most of the time. The short answer to your question is about £1,500.

It seems that often the weakest link in a video is actually the sound, not the picture. Any tips on that in terms of where and how to record the sound?
You are right, it's the area most ignored. Particularly with a script-based video, and unless you are making pop promos, the script is the key. Using the camera's microphone is always a mistake – you have to use a separate microphone. Have someone at the shoot whose only job is to check the audio. Also, never use the 'automatic' setting on the audio level – take the time to set it properly for each take, and always use headphones to listen as you record. If you get the audio right at the shoot then you can do anything you like in the edit. If it's wrong at the shoot you will never recover it.

You've worked with professional actors and presenters and also non-professionals who act as spokespeople – what's your thinking about which is better, or when each one is appropriate?
The professional will make anything sound credible; the non-professional can only do that if they know their topic and are focused on the message they want to give. A great example is Stephen Hawking. His voice isn't always easy to understand but you put up with it because he's such a visionary thinker. No one would dream of using an actor to voice his words.

Some people might want to consider doing a video blog, and I'm recommending that they commit to some kind of regular schedule. Any observations on how much work goes into that?
I feel I can't really comment as I could not do it, but if you are the kind of person who can – coherently – sum things up on a day-to-day basis, then sure. A video blog should be done regularly – once a week, once a day, once a month. I would suggest that at least five times the final duration of the piece is spent on preparation, and about three times in recording. You don't want to spend ages editing this kind of thing so it's best to get it right before you step in front of the camera.

Beyond what you've already covered, what are the most common mistakes you see in business-related videos and how could they be avoided?
I think it's all the same things you talk about in your writing workshops: tell the audience what they need to hear, not what you or your company want to say.

Any other tips?
Don't be scared to ask for help. If you can't afford a proper lighting guy then call one up and offer a small payment for his advice. Take your time. Watch TV – see what works and what does not. Finally, allow time for the editing process. We reckon on five minutes of finished programme for every day of editing, and you won't be that fast.

Distributing your podcast or vlog

When you have edited your podcast or vlog, you can host it on your own website and also make it available through iTunes and via a distribution method called RSS feeds. If you make a video that you hope will go viral, you can put it on YouTube and other sharing sites. As Richard Tierney mentioned (see page 146), when you post a video on these sites be sure you are not incorporating copyrighted music that you don't have permission to use. A site called tubemogul.com allows you to send your videos to many sites at once, after you have registered one time with each of them.

Finally, the warnings about blogs apply equally to podcasts, vlogs and videos – it's all too easy to let something slip that would have been better left unsaid, or to distribute something almost instantly that, upon reflection, needed further editing, so review all material carefully before you release it.

Your turn

To help you decide whether producing a blog, vlog, podcast, or one-off video is right for you business, jot down your answers to the following questions:

1 For the kind of information or entertainment that is relevant to your business and that your customers would value, which format do you think would be most appropriate – blog, vlog, podcast or viral video? (Of course, you can choose more than one.)

---

2 How often would you be prepared to post on your blog or vlog and/or produce a podcast?

---

3 Who is the person in your business most qualified and capable of doing this, or would you want to outsource it?

As with an e-bulletin, it's a good idea to produce a dummy edition or two to get a feel for how much work this entails and to get some independent feedback. As the cliché says, there's only one chance to make a first impression, so it's best to make any mistakes on the practice versions before going live with the real thing.

Don't forget that if this all sounds like too much work, there is another option: advertising on somebody else's blog, vlog or podcast. *Investor's Business Daily* reported in July 2008 that after having placed adverts with websites and search engines, more advertisers are starting to spread their advertising money to audio and video podcasts in order to reach certain consumers. Such advertisers include Audible, a part of Amazon.com that sells audio books, an online dating site called Geek2Geek.com and Dixie Consumer Products, makers of disposable tableware products. If you are trying to reach a well-defined target population, there's a very good chance that a blog, vlog or podcast is already out there for them. The sites should be able to give you exact figures for how many unique visitors they get, how many people download their podcast and so on. Most of them will be happy to earn a bit of extra money from an advert and they may be open to some kind of arrangement that pays based on results.

However, you have no control over what is written or said on someone else's website. If the blogger or podcaster decides to make a political statement that upsets a lot of people, for instance, some of that annoyance may rub off on you if your advert is on the site. Before you commit to an advert, track the blog or podcast for a while. Discuss any concerns you have with the person producing it – if the fit isn't right, look for another option.

Article marketing

You can write new articles or combine or expand some of your blog posts and ezine content to turn them into articles to distribute over the internet via sites such as **www.ezinearticles.com**. They welcome material about almost any subject, ideally with a length of 400–750 words. These must be articles, not press releases, advertisements, sales letters, promotional copy or blatant and excessive self-promotion and hype.

People who go to the site can read or download the articles and use them on their own websites, as long as they agree also to run the resource box at the end of each article. This box tells you who wrote the article and a little bit about the author, and it can include up to two links – for instance, to your website or blog. There is no charge for posting or downloading articles. The more you post, the more exposure you will get. The site shows how many people read or downloaded each of your articles, so you will get a good idea of which topics are of greatest interest. Naturally, you can use these sites as a source of material to add to your own website or blog as well.

Email marketing

Another option is to get people to sign up to get emails from you, usually in exchange for some kind of incentive. Thereafter, instead of sending them an e-bulletin on a regular basis, you send them a message whenever you have anything to say. The general consensus is that people will be happy to keep receiving your emails if you give them informational content rather than a hard sales message. A company called TestCountry, which sells medical testing kits, assumed that was the case. Its president, Serhat Pala, told *Marketing Sherpa*: 'From what we knew about our customers, we thought that they didn't want to get overly promotional emails. So we sent them content that was very informative and related to a featured product in the message.'

However rather than continuing to assume, TestCountry decided to test. It used a method you'll read about in Chapter Nine called a split test, which saw two versions of a message go to 20,000 subscribers each. The company kept the style and look of the messages as similar as possible, but one had a subject line that read, 'Prostate Cancer: Are you at risk? Find out today' while the other one's subject line was 'Save 5 per cent on your next TestCountry order'. The result: the promotion-heavy email was opened by twice as many people as opened the educational one. It produced five times more revenue per delivered email. While the company will continue to send educational content at times, these results have shifted their strategy towards the promotional messages. The results will not be the same for every list, of course, so the moral of the story isn't to start using a harder sell but to test what works best with your customers and go with that.

Internet marketing gurus differ in their opinions on how often you can email your list with sales pitches before they unsubscribe. Some companies actually email as often as once a day and even use tricks, like saying there was a glitch and that some people didn't receive the message so they're sending it out again, in order to expose the list to the same message twice. Needless to say, these methods are not popular with everyone. The only rule is that as long as people perceive value in what you send them, they'll stick with you. If you flood them with messages with nothing in it for them, they'll desert you.

If it's a sales message you're sending, it will be more appealing if there is a specific discount or benefit for ordering right away. If you are using an occasion, there should be a genuine reason behind it, such as a damaged or returned stock promotion or a limited quantity offer – for example, the last few copies of an earlier edition or product line. I receive lots of marketing emails that say things like, 'It's my birthday, but I'm giving *you* the present!' or 'Our crazy manager is slashing prices, buy quickly before our accountants catch up with him!' These quickly go into the virtual bin, as does a little chunk of whatever credibility that company had with me in the first place.

Mobile marketing

Marketing via messages to mobile phones is still a relatively new phenomenon and it's not yet clear what the boundaries are. We are already so wedded to our mobiles that many will not welcome the intrusion of commercial messages – unless the 'what's in it for me?' factor is strong. For instance, the Nintendo wii has been hard to get for quite a while, so someone who signed up for a waiting list might be happy to receive a call when a new shipment has come in. One of the pioneering users of mobile marketing was the Democrats in the United States, who announced Barack Obama's choice of his running mate via text messages to a huge number of his supporters who had requested to be contacted. The useful byproduct was gathering all those numbers to use again – for instance, to conduct polls or to invite people to campaign events in their area or to remind them to vote on Election Day.

On our website (**www.forentrepreneursbooks.com**) you'll find information on the latest aspects of mobile marketing. For now, however, the key point is that this is a medium that will allow you to have a very personal relationship with the recipients, but that overusing or misusing it has the potential to annoy them more than any other marketing method.

Social media

The best way to discover how businesses are using sites like MySpace and Facebook is to spend a few hours exploring them. If you go to these sites and take their tours you'll probably get ideas of your own, but to get you started here are a few ways you can use Facebook (and similar services):

→ Join existing Facebook Groups that relate to your line of business.

→ Start a Facebook Group and invite customers and other users to join.

→ Create a Facebook blog.

→ Use free Facebook Marketplace classified ads.

→ Use Facebook to invite other users to events that you stage or host.

As mentioned before, these sites are not right for a hard sell. Other than the entertainment sector, such as film studios, bands and fashion, relatively few UK businesses have embraced social networking for business purposes. Although a 2008 study by Survey Sampling International showed that 51 per cent of UK businesspeople belong to social networks, most said they used them for connecting with friends and colleagues rather than for marketing or brand awareness.

However, there's another way to utilise these sites. In many cases they give you access to your target group. By reading forums that relate to your area of business interest you can find out what your target group is thinking, what they're worried about and what they need. By posting in forums, you can establish yourself as an authority in your field. You may also be able to find the influencers who can spread your message via word of mouth and get clues as to trends that affect your business. While it's possible to waste many hours just looking up old friends on these sites, or aimlessly following various amusing but meaningless links, if you have a specific objective in mind, they can be an asset. Take a tour, check out the many groups and see whether any of them might be relevant to your business.

There are social networks that cater to businesspeople and promote online networking, and we'll look at those in some detail in Chapter Ten. For now, however, think of two or three ways that you might benefit from using sites like MySpace and Facebook:

Set aside an hour or two to have a look around a couple of these sites. From a business perspective, what did you spot that was interesting? What turned you off?

Do it yourself

If you think that the groups on sites like Facebook and MySpace are too big and you'd like to set up your own, more modest, social network, you can do this via ning.com. The groups there range from 'Doodlekisses' for fans of Labrador-poodle crossbreeds, to 'Skydiver network' for parachutists, to Sta.rtup Biz for entrepreneurs. You can put your logo or other image at the top of your network's home page and easily add text and widgets, events listings, a discussion forum, videos and slide shows and photos. Each member gets a profile page. It is also possible to create subgroups within the network. It's free as long as you allow Ning to put adverts on your Ning site. If you prefer not to have adverts, the monthly fee is about £10. You can also pay a bit extra to use your own domain name for your network (rather than one that includes .ning in the name) or to get more storage and extra bandwidth.

Your website

Websites are now such an accepted part of marketing that it's tempting to put them into the next chapter on old media. For that reason, and because both the technical and aesthetic aspects of websites are complex topics and have many books dedicated to them, I'll only cover a few points here. First, it's vital to know what you want your website to do. Websites serve the following four main functions:

→ **To make it easy for people to find you**. If they type your name or the name of your business into a search engine like Google, they should be taken to a website that tells them what you do, who you are, where you are and how to contact you.

→ **To reflect the benefits of what you offer**. Once more, we return to the importance of communicating to the potential customer what's in it for them – this should be clear to anyone perusing your site.

→ **To build trust and credibility**. One way to do this is to include testimonials on the site. Video testimonials, where we can see the people making the statements, and maybe even a video of the results of using your product or service, are the strongest. Next is audio, then text. If you do use video or audio, it's a good idea to have at least part of the testimonial in text form as well, for people who prefer to get information in that format. There are also more subtle aspects to this, such as whether the colour scheme and the graphics used on the site encourage confidence. For a children's entertainer a site full of cartoons and splashy bright colours would be appropriate, whereas for a financial adviser it would not.

→ **To get the visitor to take action**. What this action will be varies and is sometimes a combination of things, such as:

— signing up for your e-bulletin by leaving their name and email address;
— requesting some report or other incentive product, again by leaving their details;
— contacting you for further information;
— buying your product or service on the site.

Most of the time your minimum objective will be to capture a name and email address so that you can, with their permission, continue to market to them. This means that you will have not one but several opportunities to turn them into customers.

If you are selling products on your website it's vital that you make it easy for people to pay securely via credit card or an online payments system such as PayPal. You must also give them contact information so they feel confident that if something goes wrong with the payment, they will be able to contact you easily.

With the above characteristics in mind, take a fresh, dispassionate look at your website. Can you think of three things to improve about the content?

_____

_____

_____

'The haggle button'

A few years ago the online retailer West Coast Golf found it had a big problem. On its website it was not allowed to show prices lower than the industry's minimum advertised price, but in competing stores the salespeople were allowed to negotiate a lower price. The West Coast Golf site invited people to phone up to discuss prices, but there were few takers. Then the company hit upon the idea of putting a 'let's haggle' button on the website. It invited visitors to the site to contact the company via email to make a deal. As reported on the *Marketing Sherpa* website, it worked. However, it took a lot of emails back and forth. Next, the company hired a programmer to write an automated price-negotiation program, labelled 'Make an Offer'. The program includes an acceptable range of reduced prices. If customers offer a price within this range they get a message saying, 'Accepted price: [the amount].' If the offer is too low, the message is, 'We are sorry. Your bid of [the amount] is lower than we can sell this item for. Please try another bid or another product.'

The company sales doubled in the first three months that the button was on the website. In the first full year it was in operation, site revenue went up 376 per cent. Whether or not such a button is appropriate for your product or service, it's a great example of creative marketing. It also illustrates what happens when you give the consumer some power, as well as an experience they are likely to talk about.

Will people find your site?

Another major concern is how to make your site easy to find. Over the past few years the sometimes dark art of SEO, search engine optimisation, has sprung up. This relates to what keywords you need to put on your site, and where you need to put them, in order to attract the search engine 'spiders' that are constantly roaming the internet and cataloguing its contents. If your site appears on the first page or two of search results on Google or the other major search engines, you have struck marketing gold. Naturally, this is everybody's objective and can be very difficult to achieve. You can hire SEO specialists, but it's not a one-time cost since the search engines keep changing their methods of ranking sites. Here are a few practical tips you can implement yourself.

Start with a good web address

It is ideal if your url (your web address) specifies what you sell or do. This makes it easier for the search engines, which look for keywords in domain names. It also helps because quite a few people type something like **www.antiquemaps.com** directly into a search window on the assumption that such a site exists.

In the case of one of my books, *Your Writing Coach*, I was able to buy the url, **www.yourwritingcoach.com**. In the case of another, *Focus: The Power of Targeted Thinking*, www.focus.com was already gone and using the entire title of the book would have made for a very long url. Instead, I chose the best alternative I could find, **www.focusquick.com**, because at least it has the word 'focus' in it, and it's easy to remember. If you originally housed a website at a nondescript name (e.g. **www.joebloggsproducts.co.uk**) and you find a more descriptive url (e.g. **www.antiquemaps.com**), you can buy the new name and easily set it up to redirect people automatically to your old site. One example, cited in *Business Week* magazine, is a business owner who saw her visitor numbers increase dramatically when she changed her site name from **www.expressionspd.com**, for the name of her business, Expressions Photo Design, to **www.ilovephotogifts.com**.

Use keywords, but not excessively

Keywords are the phrases that people search for. If your titles, subtitles and text include keywords that describe what you do, your ranking will improve. However, if you go overboard to the point where your text no longer sounds natural but rather like one long advert with certain keywords repeated endlessly, the search engines will assume you are 'stuffing', which is the equivalent of spam, and you will actually be penalised.

Add new content regularly

Search engines like websites that add new content, which is one excellent reason for hosting your blog, vlog or podcast on your own site. If you allow comments on your blog, those also count as new content.

If you publish an e-bulletin, you can also add it to the archives of your site a month after it goes out to your subscribers, or you can add only part of it if you want to give subscribers the feeling that they won't get the full content any other way than by subscribing. If you publish articles on an article distribution site, also add them on your own website. If you make some changes to the material, the search engines will not consider it duplicate, which again can help your search ranking.

If you would like to keep your site relatively lean, you can add content for a limited time. Influence expert Kevin Hogan does this on his site, **www.kevinhogan.com**. In his e-bulletin he mentions the featured articles on his website and says they will be up for a limited time only (using the appeal to scarcity). That sends readers to the site to read them before they disappear, which means he's getting lots of visitors on a regular basis – and while they're there, naturally they also are exposed to all of his products and services.

Having photos and other graphics can make a site more appealing, but search engines can't see videos or images so be sure to caption them.

Toolkit

If you need someone to construct a website for you, consider using an outsourcing service like RentACoder or Elance. These are services on which you specify what you need and then suppliers from around the world bid on the work. They are explained more fully in Chapter Eleven.

Get links to your site

A link is simply a word or phrase or image that people can click on in order to be taken to your website. The more genuine links you have coming in to your site, the better, especially if they are one-way – that is, from sites to which you don't have links on your site. Why should other sites link to yours? Perhaps because you have great content that their visitors would find of interest, or you host a great video or have some kind of tool. For instance, on a fitness site it might be a tool that allows people to enter information about themselves and get their estimated body-fat percentage. Other possibilities include contests, free reports and reviews. Naturally, the people most likely to link to you for any of these will not be your direct competitors but businesses that may be complementary in some way. A site about nutrition probably wouldn't mind linking to a site about exercise. A site selling DIY materials might be willing to link to one that features videos about how to do simple home repairs. If you find a site that links to your competitors, ask them to link to you as well.

You can also create links to your site yourself – for instance, in electronically distributed press releases or print press releases that are quoted on websites. Similarly, you should include a link to your website in the 'about' box at the end of any articles you write for sites like ezinearticles.com.

Avoid any marketers who offer you 'black hat' search engine optimisation. These are methods of trying to fool the search engines by creating bogus links in any number of ways. The search engines usually catch up with these methods sooner or later and if they find you using them you will suddenly have a situation where nobody can find you via the search engine. For the same reason, avoid buying links.

With these factors in mind, can you identify two or three additional aspects of your website you might want to change?

_____

_____

_____

_____

'Is the pizza Polish?'

In 2003 the Italian government decided to commission a national tourism portal where visitors could book hotel rooms and also learn about the country, including its national dishes and its great artists, writers and film-makers. The website went live in February 2007. Unfortunately it was riddled with errors. The first name of world-renowned film director Federico Fellini was listed as 'Gioacchino.' Napoleon's birthplace was listed as Elba instead of Corsica. The list of typical seafood dishes from the region of Marche included pork roast with prunes, a dish popular in Poland. A logo that cost £80,000 to design was so unpopular that it was withdrawn. The site was based on two databases, which were not compatible. After six months, the portal was shut down. It had cost more than £35 million.

The following are some of the reasons for the fiasco:

→ Too many cooks spoil the spaghetti. Several government ministries, 20 regional governments and a variety of travel agency and hotel owner groups all had a say. There was no one strong voice directing the effort.

→ There was too much money available. With no constraints in terms of funds and time, many aspects of the project spiralled out of control. One expert, quoted in the *Wall Street Journal*, said the whole thing could have been done well for under £800,000.

→ It was based on too many (sometimes conflicting) technologies, and their incompatibility didn't become obvious until the website was completed.

All of these are useful warnings for anybody constructing a website. Before you start, have a clear vision of what you want. Even if you allocate the work to several people or companies according to the required skills, it's important for there to be one person in charge who makes sure that everything that is done is compatible and is coming in on time. It's also vital to test everything so the bugs, glitches and mistakes that creep into almost every project will be discovered and corrected before the public ever gets to see the site.

Paying for popularity

You have the option of paying to be found by placing adverts on the search engine pages. The primary method of doing this is using 'pay-per-click' advertising. You bid on a search term and if you are the highest bidder the search engine places a link to your site and a line of text at the top of the paid section of their search results page. Let's say you sell antique maps on your website. You can bid on the term 'antique maps' and the price will be determined by how many others want that term and what they are willing to pay for it. The more generic the term, the more in demand, and therefore the more expensive it is likely to be. You may be shocked at how much some companies are willing to pay for a particular term. After all, getting someone to click on the link doesn't mean they'll actually buy anything or even leave their email address when they get there. The reason that some keywords go for so much is that companies are looking at the potential lifetime value of the customers they attract. If you have only one product that sells for, say, £29, it doesn't make sense to spend £30 attracting each buyer. However, if you have a whole pipeline of products or services that you hope to sell, some of which may cost thousands, then it may.

Let's look at the numbers. A business coach might have an initial product – e.g., an e-book on how to be more productive. Of every 2,000 people who click the link to that site, 100 buy the e-book for £12. Of those 100, 20 also opt to buy a multimedia product on overcoming pro-crastination, which sells for £97. And of those 20, three eventually opt for a personal coaching programme, which sells for £250 per month, and they stay for an average of six months. The total gross income from those 2,000 clicks will be £7,640, or £3.82 per click. Obviously it doesn't make sense to spend that much per click, otherwise there will be no profit, but you can see that in this instance it could make sense to pay as much as 50p per click or even a bit more.

Naturally, when you are just starting to use the internet you have no way of knowing what the conversion rate – the percentage of people who buy – will be for every stage of your product or service pipeline, so it's better to be conservative and not invest heavily until you start getting some results.

A good strategy is to come up with as many possible variations on a term as you can and check how often each is being searched for and what the price for it is. Instead of 'antique maps', it may be less costly and equally effective for you to bid on the term 'old maps.' If you specialise, it could make sense to go for the term 'antique European maps'.

As you can probably tell, this is a complex topic. You can find out more on the Google site, under Google AdWords; and our website, **www.forentrepreneursbooks.com**, will provide links to more detailed sources of information. For now, jot down half a dozen keywords and phrases that might be most relevant to your product or service:

_____

_____

_____

Do a search for these and notice which websites come up on the first page. Use several different search engines – Google, Yahoo! and MSN are the most popular. Are the sites that appear your direct competitors? What's different about what you offer? How might you refine your keywords so they would be more specific to your product or service? Jot down any alternatives you come up with:

_____

_____

_____

When things go wrong

The good news is that social media, blogs, podcasts, and even your website allow for interaction with lots of people. That's also the bad news. Someone may bad-mouth your product or service on a website forum (maybe even your own) or in the comments on your blog or podcast. Your first impulse may be to try to get rid of these comments or at least to censor them. That's usually not a good idea. Of course, if the comments are libellous or pornographic or stated in language that people would find offensive, they should be removed. But if they are simply critical or negative opinions, generally it's best to leave them. Naturally you can answer them, but if they are stated in emotional terms don't stoop to the same level.

If the person has a grievance you can set right, perhaps with a refund or an apology for service that could have been better, that's the best way to proceed. If you respond quickly and calmly, usually you can turn a critic back into a fan. By leaving the evidence of your positive response on the site you show others how quickly you act when you're in the wrong. That instils confidence and trust and is much better than trying to hide the fact that you're not perfect. In corporate history and politics, too, the greatest damage has been done not when someone has made an error, but when they have denied it or tried to cover it up.

Of course, in some cases your critic may be totally irrational. Sadly there are people who are angry with the world and look for a person or company to try to blame for their woes. Again, resist the temptation to respond emotionally. Instead, respond with a message along the lines of, 'We're sorry, we understand that you feel your criticism is justified, but our efforts to meet you halfway have failed and it looks like we will just have to agree to disagree.' If further negative comments appear, don't argue. Without the satisfaction of a fight, the person probably will move on and find a new target.

If negative comments appear on other sites, respond quickly and unemotionally. If you feel the comments step beyond the limits of free speech into slander or libel, request that they be removed. I did this with Amazon, when someone with a novel with a title vaguely similar to the title of one of my non-fiction books left a 'review', ranting about how I'd stolen his title and using extremely derogatory language about my national origins. I checked a few other books with somewhat similar titles and saw that he had spread his bile to them as well. A request to Amazon to remove these remarks was honoured quickly. Eventually his book listing, which featured some obviously fake favourable reviews, was deleted as well. In extreme cases you may need to consult a solicitor, but most of the time that won't be necessary. In order to be sure that you're aware of what's being said about you on the internet, use the Google Alert feature described in Chapter Five.

How Dell did it

Dell, the computer company, learned the hard way the importance of allocating resources to dealing with complaints and negative comments online. Once noted for excellent customer service, it had gradually come to take its customers for granted. The disgruntled buyers vented their frustration online in large numbers. Now Dell is turning things around. It has 42 employees whose job it is to be on Facebook, Twitter and other social media to keep track of what people are saying and to deal quickly with any complaints. The company also has added blogs and message boards to its sites so that dissatisfied customers can discuss their problems directly rather than complaining on internet forums. Furthermore, it has created a site where customers can give their ideas as to what features would be useful on future models. The company has acted on several of them, such as keyboards that light up in the dark and a greater choice of case colours. Finally, it has established a site where customers can post their tech problems or questions and where other forum users can help them with advice. Not only does this create a friendly feel around the Dell name, but also it cuts down on the number of tech support calls the company has to deal with, which saves it money.

Your turn

Jot down any ideas you have on how you could use your website, social media or other new media approaches to help improve your customer relations:

_____

_____

_____

_____

_____

Marketing power boost

Out of the mouths of babes

It used to be said that if you wanted someone who knew how to program a video recorder you should ask an eight-year-old. These days the same is true if you want to know what's up and coming on the internet. Once every three to six months, convene a small focus group of children aged 10 to 16 (which should be supervised by at least two responsible adults). You can recruit your own children and their friends, or those of your employees, colleagues or relations.

Provide some snacks and get them to tell you about the newest and coolest things happening with social media or the internet in general. If you don't feel at ease leading the discussion get someone closer to their age group to do it. Brief this person as to the kind of information you are seeking. Pay as much attention to what the youngsters talk about during the breaks as when answering your questions. It's when they're not trying to tell you what they think you want to hear that you'll get the most useful information. If you're very brave, ask them to critique your website and other online marketing materials. Even if they're not your target group their fresh thinking might yield some useful ideas. This strategy is also useful because in this realm, often whatever children are using today adults will be using tomorrow. Gather together all the topics that came up in this meeting. By yourself or with some colleagues, brainstorm whether and how any of these ideas and trends might be useful for your marketing.

Web bonus

At our website, **www.forentrepreneursbooks.com**, click on the 'Marketing for Entrepreneurs' button. On the link for Chapter Seven you'll find links to half a dozen successful podcasts and vlogs that represent a variety of content, approaches, lengths and formats, as well as to some skilfully done business-related videos that have achieved wide distribution.

Key points

→ New media offer powerful marketing channels and ways to establish trust and credibility.

→ E-bulletins and email campaigns are low-cost ways to reach customers regularly.

→ A blog allows you to add content frequently.

→ A podcast is the equivalent of your own business radio programme.

→ A vlog (video blog) adds moving images and is easy to distribute.

Next steps

What action will you take to apply the information in this chapter? By when will you do it?

_____

_____

_____

_____

Old media – opportunities for contrarians

Chapter Eight

The new media get all the glory these days. There's something sexy about having a great website, having your own blog or podcast and being on top of the latest developments around social marketing. However, sometimes this leaves the mistaken impression that the old media, including newspapers, magazines, radio, television and humble media such as leaflets and posters, are dead. Nothing could be further from the truth. These are all still extremely effective marketing tools, and the fact that so many entrepreneurs are ignoring them in favour of the online world may provide you with a great opportunity. By employing a good mix of old and new media you can turbo-charge your marketing and zoom ahead of your competitors.

Your paper image

When you have decided on what you want your image and your USP to be, every message you send in any form should reflect these. This includes all the ways you communicate on paper – for instance:

→ letterhead;
→ business cards;
→ invoices;
→ mailing labels;
→ brochures and flyers;
→ catalogues or price lists;
→ press releases;
→ compliments sheets;
→ signs.

You may not think of something like letterhead as a marketing tool, but it does create an impression of your business. Sometimes the style of lettering and of illustrations becomes a defining characteristic in themselves, as in the days when artist Ralph Steadman provided his brilliant splotchy illustrations for all the Oddbins flyers and catalogues.

The logo, the font, the colours and the style of any illustrations or graphics should be consistent. Even if you have a flair for art, it's usually unwise to try to do this yourself. Get an experienced graphic designer to help you come up with a logo and make decisions about the other design elements, and stick to them from then on. If money is tight, check your local art colleges for promising students in graphic design. They may give you a good rate in exchange for having something to put in their portfolios, but make sure they've had enough experience to know how to prepare the materials for printing. Shop around for printers because their rates can vary a great deal, especially during sales promotions. My local print shop has a half-price sale on a different product every month. One month it will be flyers, the next it will be letterhead. I always wait for the specials and then order enough to see me through until the next sale.

Naturally, all your contact information should be on everything you have printed, as well as the url of your website and, if hosted separately, the address of your blog, vlog or podcast – if you have any of those. If you publish an e-bulletin, note that on your printed materials as well, with instructions on how people can sign up for it.

Sometimes simple works

Putting a little card in the window of your local post office qualifies as a classic marketing method, and probably one that would be dismissed by most entrepreneurs as unprofessional. Not so fast! In the *Marketability eBulletin*, Helen Moore told of a company that opened a new self-storage facility in Hampshire. It was gearing up for an expensive advertising campaign, but in the meantime put a card in a local post office window for 50p per week. After six weeks, it had generated £250,000 worth of business.

Another method is to print up postcards with some kind of puzzle, intriguing visual, cartoon or other interesting content on the front – relevant to your business, of course. On the back you can have a special offer and contact information, as well as the addresses of your website, blog and podcast. If the information on the postcard is useful, such as 'ten tips' or 'five ways to…', people will keep it around longer. Publicity expert Marcia Yudkin came up with a creative twist on this by creating a ten-instalment mini-seminar on colourful postcards.

You can also print flyers or posters with similar information. As always, make the 'what's in it for me?' quotient high – people won't put a poster on the wall if all it's doing is advertising your business.

You can apply to a variety of print materials the methods of copywriting outlined earlier in this book. A catchy headline followed by an explanatory subheading, followed by a body of text that dramatically reveals the benefits of your product or service and finishes with a call to action, is a reliable structure.

With postcards, flyers and posters you may be able to find non-competing companies that have similar materials and are willing to do a swap – you place their materials at your locations and they place yours at theirs.

Promote with giveaways

Merchandise like pens and little puzzles with your company's name on may seem old-fashioned and not very interesting, but go to any convention and notice how many well-paid people snatch up these kinds of goodies to take home. They won't have a big impact by themselves but may be worth considering as part of your overall marketing package. If you do go for something like this, hunt around for an item that is different and memorable, rather than just another pen or key ring. For instance, you can get custom jigsaw puzzles made, or custom messages that go inside fortune cookies. Some of the most popular printed promotional items, as reported in a survey by printing.com, are:

→ wall planners;
→ desk calendars;
→ case calendars (one card per month in an acrylic case);
→ pocket calendars;
→ mobile phone holders;
→ hanging calendars.

Even these traditional items can be made more interesting. For example, if you are creating a calendar, avoid the usual scenic landscapes and think about what images would appeal to your niche.

Sites like clipart.com, iStock and en.fotolia.com offer you a choice of millions of photos and illustrations at very reasonable prices.

Use surprise discounts

A simple way to make buying things from you more fun is to give an instant, surprise 10 or 20 per cent discount to every tenth or twenty-fifth customer. This works even if you don't advertise it. Imagine how delighted you would be if you went into a shop, made a purchase and suddenly were told you were getting 20 per cent off the price. It's probably something you'd talk about to your colleagues and friends.

Print ads

Print ads run the gamut from a full page in the *Sunday Times* down to a classified ad in your local church bulletin, and it's not always the case that the more expensive advert is the better one. As with all other marketing tools, you must first decide which medium is best for reaching your target customers. If your product would appeal primarily to people who play the violin, for example, it makes more sense to spend your money on several adverts in classical music magazines than on one advert in a general circulation magazine. The kind of print publications you may want to consider include:

→ local newspapers;
→ newsletters of professional groups;
→ theatre programmes;
→ free sheets (newspapers that are given away);
→ church newsletters;
→ newsletters of social groups;
→ specialist magazines (for instance, those that cater to people with particular hobbies or skills).

Larger publications have rate cards that indicate the prices of various sizes of adverts such as 1/16 of a page, 1/8 of a page and so forth. Often there is room for negotiation, so don't hesitate to haggle. One bargaining method to use is to say that you want to place an advert once to find out how effective it is to advertise in this publication, and if it works well you will be running the ad on a regular basis at their full rates. How receptive they are to such offers depends partly on how much ad space remains unsold as their next publication date approaches.

Smaller publications may be even more amenable to making a deal. You may be able to set up some kind of barter arrangement if you have a product or service they could find useful. In some situations they may be open to taking payment on results – that is, a commission on the sales made through the advert running in their publication. In that case they will want to have the orders sent to them initially so they can be sure that you are reporting the number of sales accurately.

Beware the cleverness trap

While cleverness and doing something different are highly recommended, sometimes an advert can go wrong by trying too hard to be clever. At the moment, Sony is running ads for its Vaio line of laptops with this headline: 'Ever wished your screen was clearer? Maybe you're a VAIO.' I don't know about you, but on first reading I interpret this as meaning if you're a VAIO computer, you wish your screen was clearer. Of course, that's the opposite of what Sony intends (and I happen to think that, leaving Apple laptops aside, the VAIOs are the coolest ones around). But by using that ambiguous heading, it is sending a message that at best is confusing and at worst is completely opposite to what they intend. Furthermore, the visual that goes with this is a murky shot of one of Sony's laptops … with the screen facing away from us. How is that going to make us associate this brand with a richer, brighter picture? This would be understandable in a newspaper ad, since the reproduction quality wouldn't do justice to the screen image, but this advert is running in glossy colour magazines.

It just goes to prove that having a major advertising budget and undoubtedly an expensive ad agency behind you doesn't mean you'll get it right – and, of course, having a small budget and only your own creativity to fall back on doesn't mean you'll get it wrong.

'The fake sumo'

HSBC, which calls itself the world's local bank, ran a series of print and billboard advertisements showing a sumo wrestler with the headline, 'Fixed savings rates that won't budge.' The problem: instead of a genuine Japanese sumo wrestler, they used an overweight white man dressed up and be-wigged to look like one. Some members of Britain's Japanese community took offence to the fact that the man's skin had been darkened and his eyes made up so they looked narrower. HSBC's spokesperson defended the advert and said the mascara extending from the outside of the eye was 'there to emphasise the eyes, reduce glare and cover lines', not to alter the ethnicity of the model. They also defended the use of make up and the change in his skin tone.

Regardless of the intention, the ad is culturally insensitive. Probably it would have been more effective for the company to say immediately, 'We meant no offence, but we got it wrong, we've pulled all those ads, and we apologise to our Japanese friends and customers.' Generally, one sincere 'sorry' stops controversy in its tracks, while defensive statements only prolong it.

Coupon marketing

The use of discount coupons has declined in recent times, but has started to make a comeback as the economy falters. As well as print coupons, consider downloadable ones.

One survey carried out in America by ICOM Information and Communications revealed that almost 80 per cent of people aged 18–34 are more likely to use coupons if they can be downloaded. Using coupons to give temporary price reductions gives you more flexibility than just making across the board price cuts.

Trade show stands

For some businesses getting exposure at trade shows is an effective marketing tool. After all, it's one of the few times that customers come directly to you in great numbers. Of course, it's also a situation in which they will probably be able to go with equal ease to your competitors if they also have stands. There are a few key points to consider when signing up for a trade show.

Location, location, location

Sign up early so you don't end up being stuck in some obscure corner of the exhibitions hall. Being near the entrance is good, being on a corner is good and being near the food area is good. Being near a very popular exhibitor who is not a direct competitor also can be good, in that you will get some of the spillover.

Take a troubleshooter

If there are any problems with the electrical supply or the furniture hire, or any technical issues, you don't want to have to leave the stand to deal with them. Take along a colleague who can handle such matters, leaving you or another colleague to do the meet-and-greet.

Do something different to draw visitors

How many mundane stands have you passed by? You know the kind: a poster or two on the walls; a fishbowl into which to drop your business card in order to win a boring prize; and someone wearing a polyester jacket and a hungry look, hoping you'll venture in to pick up a standard brochure or two to stuff into your plastic bag and throw away as soon as you get home. It doesn't work. Some things that do work are:

→ celebrity spokespersons;
→ draws for truly covetable prizes (think iPod or iPhone, for instance);
→ the first chance to see a truly revolutionary product in action;
→ handouts with information that visitors can really use (not just sales pitches);

Marketing for Entrepreneurs

- → food (but check the rules first as many exhibition halls forbid it for health and safety reasons, or because they don't want to hurt the sales of their food concessions);
- → someone doing something interesting;
- → knowledgeable people staffing the stands and offering to give free advice;
- → an unusual experience for the visitor.

In other words, your booth needs to have a USP, ideally one that connects with the USP of your business. Perhaps you remember the 'Marketing Hall of Fame' example of Pioneer televisions (see page 34), where the USP was the deep blacks on the plasma TV screens and all the marketing materials handed out were black. I could imagine that if Pioneer were to take space at a trade fair, it might construct a mock tunnel into which visitors would be guided one by one, creating a sense of mystery. Inside it would be pitch black, until suddenly one of its big plasma screens sprang to life with a brilliant image, maybe something very funny or very scary in order to evoke an emotional response that could be heard by others waiting to go in. Don't you think that would create a huge amount of interest? If you exhibit at trade shows, what could you do differently that would make your stand more interesting? Jot down any ideas that occur to you:

_____

_____

_____

Use the opportunity to check out the competition

If you don't want to do this yourself, send a spy to pick up their literature, ask them questions and listen to their sales pitches. Ideally, use a friend rather than an employee so they don't have to lie when asked who they work for. Analyse all the information that was gathered in order to work out what they do better than you. Can you learn from how they do things? Also consider what they do badly. Can you exploit that weakness in order to win over some of their customers? Of course, you must be prepared for the fact that they will probably do the same thing.

Use the opportunity to forge alliances

Check out which companies at the show make a good impression. Chat with them and explore whether it may be possible to work together in some way. You can start at the show by referring some of your visitors to their stand, when appropriate, and ask them to do the same. If it seems that there is scope for more collaboration, set up a time to discuss it away from the hurly-burly of the show.

Keep track of your visitors and what they want

If you chat with someone and get their card, as soon as they step away note on the back of the card what you discussed and any information that could be useful when you follow up. To help you remember who they were, jot down a few descriptive words: 'the tall, bald man', 'the woman with the dolphin broach', or whatever.

Build a database

Create a list of all the people you met so that you preserve their email and physical addresses. This makes it easier when you come to follow up.

Follow up

The whole exercise will have been largely wasted if you don't follow up on the leads you have gathered. However, rather than giving them the sales pitch they'll be expecting, send them something they will find useful – an article, a report, a sample or anything else that will be a pleasant surprise. They may then take the initiative to get back to you to thank you, and that will advance the contact further. If you don't hear from them, you can ring them to ask whether they received it. Use the database to stay in touch. Someone who is not ready to buy right now may well be in the market six months or a year down the line.

Direct mail

Direct mail simply means anything you send directly to a potential customer. This can include sales letters, catalogues and postcards.

Direct mail has the following three drawbacks:

→ If you're mailing to a list of names that isn't current or well targeted, you will have wasted your money.

→ Many people just throw away anything they consider 'junk mail', which again leads to waste, both environmentally and in terms of your spending.

→ When you add up the cost of printing, envelopes and especially postage, it's an expensive way to get your message across.

However there are also three factors on the plus side:

→ Because so many people are now using the internet to advertise, a letter stands out more.

→ If potential customers are interested but not ready to buy, they may keep your letter, flyer or catalogue and use it later.

→ People who are not interested may pass your material on to a friend, family member or colleague who is.

Who to mail to

The list of people to whom you are sending material may have been generated by you. For instance, it could be people who have used a coupon in your newspaper or magazine advert, or a button and form on your website to ask for a catalogue to be sent to them. Obviously this kind of list is ideal because it's another example of 'permission marketing', addressing your marketing to people who have asked for it.

If you don't have a list of your own, you can rent a mailing list from a list broker for direct marketing to the individual consumer or business to business. In that case you want to be sure that the list is current and relevant. Twelve per cent of the UK population changes address every year, so an old list can result in a lot of returned post. And if the list is not targeted you'll be sending your offer to people who have no interest in it. Reputable list brokers will be able to give you key data about their lists and help you select the right one. You can get lists that are segmented according to criteria such as geographical area, age, income, hobbies, gender and lifestyle – in fact, all the key elements you used when you decided who to target.

Test first

If you are planning to do a large mailing, test the list first with a randomly selected sample of names. That way, if the list turns out not to be productive, you will find out before you've committed a lot of money. Most list brokers will help you set up this kind of test.

If you are using a direct mail campaign at the same time as some other major marketing efforts, work out a way to trace where your customers are coming from. For instance, you might use a promotional code for people to quote if they phone in their order. To motivate people to cite this code, give them a small discount or some kind of bonus for doing so.

Buy or rent

You can buy a list or merely rent one. If you rent, you will be charged a fee every time you use it. The brokers include some fake names so that they get a copy of every direct mail piece that is addressed to people on their lists and can make sure it's not being used again without authorisation. However, once people have bought from you, you would add them to your own list.

Get them to read it

Lists will help you to get your message to the right people. Then it's up to you to make that message as appealing as possible, using all the methods we have discussed. The biggest hurdle can be just getting people to open the envelope. Pay attention to the direct mail you get.

What makes you decide to open one and throw another in the bin? It could be an image or message on the outside of the envelope. Some companies use hand-addressed envelopes – an expensive solution but one that does result in a much higher opening rate.

There are lots of ways to be creative about the timing and styles of direct mail. For example, JoJo Maman Bébé, which sells maternity wear and baby goods, sends out mail-order catalogues quarterly. The company discovered that sales fall off after six to twelve weeks and decided to experiment with sending follow-up postcards after two months, featuring discounts on three products from the main catalogue. A month later it sent out another postcard, this time with a 15 per cent discount code for everything in the catalogue. The result was orders averaging around £48 from an additional 1 per cent of the list. Now it sends up to five such postcards a season.

Radio ads

Radio tends to be underestimated as a marketing tool. With local commercial radio you can target at least a broad demographic group by choosing the format that is most likely to appeal to them, such as talk, jazz, pop, classical, urban, all-news or oldies gold. Within those you can also choose the time of day or night the people you want to reach are most likely to be listening. This could be as they get ready for work, as they drive to their workplace, during the day when those at home are listening while doing housework or studying, and so forth. Radio stations will be able to give you the demographics of their listeners as well as listening patterns.

The figures are impressive: according to RAJAR's figures from the second quarter of 2008, more than 45 million adults (15+) listen to the radio every week, with 31 million adults listening to commercial radio. Commercial radio takes a 77 per cent share of all local listening.

The use of voice, music and sound effects allow you to craft a message that has emotional impact as well as imparting facts. Radio is a much more personal, one-to-one experience than most other forms.

Tell them what to do

Because typically you will have only 15, 30, 45 or 60 seconds and generally listeners will be doing something else at the same time, the message needs to be succinct. As always, focus on benefits. And, as with all the other marketing methods, it's vital that you start with a clear idea of what you want people to do as a result of hearing your advert. These could include:

→ calling a phone number to get more information or to order;

→ going to a website to get more information or to order;

→ buying your product the next time they are in a shop.

People who have heard about an expensive product or service only on the radio probably will want to get more information before they buy. If you are getting them to ring a freephone number, it's essential that the people taking their calls are friendly, knowledgeable and accurate. This is the part of the chain that often lets businesses down. If you are outsourcing this service, call anonymously from time to time and ask some 'dumb' questions to find out what kind of experience your customers are having with your call centre.

They're the experts but you're the boss

Your local radio station will be able to produce your advert in-house or refer you to an agency or production company. As with television, sometimes these people are more interested in being creative for its own sake than in crafting a message that actually creates the actions you want. Humour is great but beware adverts that make people laugh but not remember what product or service was being sold. Brief your supplier to be sure they know your USP, the tone you want the advert to have (it should be consistent with the tone of the rest of your marketing materials), who you are trying to reach, the benefits you want to convey and what you want the listeners to do.

When you are judging whether a proposed radio ad is good, the UK Radio Advertising Bureau (**www.rab.co.uk**) advises using the five **I**s:

- → **Involvement**: will it draw in listeners?
- → **Identify**: will listeners know who the ad is about?
- → **Impression**: will listeners get the right impression of the brand?
- → **Information**: will the listener understand what the ad is saying?
- → **Integration**: if the ad is part of a wider campaign, will the listener make the connection?

As with print ads, it may be possible to haggle on the price of placing your radio ads, especially if you intend to buy a series of ad spots if your initial tests are positive.

Marketing Hall of Fame

The Sparhawk secret

Sparhawk Brewers is a small American brewery located in Portland, Maine. It started with a small budget and almost no name recognition. It turned to radio for a daring campaign designed to make locals aware of the brand and build a following.

The company and its agency, Pirate Radio and Television, decided to use four local stations and four phases of storytelling via its radio ads. In phase one the brewer simply introduced itself as a local, friendly business. In the next phase it added an element of conflict: supposedly the local people couldn't get Sparhawk beer because tourists were drinking most of it (Portland is a tourist spot in New England). Phase three was the solution to this supposed problem: it would introduce a secret code, which was a particular three-note whistle, that only the locals would understand. When they heard it, they would know that another batch of Sparhawk beer had been brewed and was ready for them to buy. And the final phase was a series of radio ads for fake businesses, such as Sparhawk Motors and the Sparhawk Mortuary Travel Urn. At the end of these amusing messages the whistle would be sounded, but the ads never mentioned Sparhawk beer.

By using a series of adverts the company was able to draw listeners into the story and give them an amusing 'secret' to keep. What was the result? The Canadian Radio Marketing Bureau reports that after this campaign, which was also written up in the local press, Sparhawk's sales figures were 540 per cent better than expected. Within a few weeks people on the street started whistling the 'code' at Sparhawk delivery drivers. Bar patrons used the whistle to order another Sparhawk beer. Within three months, the company had to double its production schedule twice.

This is a good example of using radio for what it does best: target a specific geographic area; use storytelling as a way to attract the attention of the target group; use a sequence of messages rather than try to do it all in one hit; and entertain while achieving the selling goals. With its fake ads and the use of the code whistle the company also followed the principle of doing something different.

You may have noticed that this campaign uses the basic elements of the 'hero's journey' you read about in Chapter Six. In this example, Sparhawk cast the listeners as the heroes. They are going along in their normal lives and then, via the phase one messages, they find out there's a new beer in town, one they might want to try. That's the call to adventure. But, as explained in phase two, there's an obstacle. Tourists are drinking all the Sparhawk, leaving none for the locals. This makes the tourists the enemy. The heroes have a wise ally: the Sparhawk brewers, who in phase three suggest a cunning plan involving a secret message. Then, in phase four, the heroes listen to a series of messages and the whistle code works, allowing them to get the prize, Sparhawk beer. Even though the whole thing obviously was tongue-in-cheek, it made an entertaining story that got the target audience involved.

Making the customer rather than the product the hero of the story was a clever strategy. It reflects the two most important concepts of marketing that have been emphasised throughout this book. First, the customer doesn't care about your product, only about what it can do for them. In this case the 'prize' was not only the experience of drinking the presumably delicious beer, but also the fun of being in on a secret. The other important marketing concept it used is the fact that we buy based on emotion. Our emotions are aroused much more by a story with a hero, an enemy and an adventure than by a set of facts and figures. And when we feel like we are part of the story, the message is even stronger.

Television ads

Television is considered the most glamorous medium. Having an ad campaign on television confers a number of advantages – for example:

- → wide reach – in one advert during a popular programme you can reach millions of people;
- → status for your business – people tend to think that companies that advertise on television must be successful;
- → status for the product being advertised – the phrase 'as seen on TV' reflects that people tend to award more credibility to things they see on television;
- → emotional impact – because you can work with moving images as well as sound, it's easier to create messages that make the audience react.

There are also some disadvantages – for example:

- → making television commercials is expensive;
- → buying television air time is expensive;
- → it's not possible to segment the audience as much as can be done with some other marketing media;
- → the advert can get lost in the clutter of ads during commercial breaks;
- → it's becoming easier for people to skip the adverts, either by muting the sound or recording the programme and then fast-forwarding past the ads when they watch.

It has to look good

When your advert is on TV it's seen in the context of programmes that have high production values, so your ad has to look good as well. While the grunge, low-budget approach can work online, especially if – as Richard Tierney pointed out in Chapter Seven – the script is strong enough, that won't do for broadcast TV. Here you need not only a good script, but also good actors, a skilled director, the right lighting, good sound, and just the right location or set. In other words, it's not a DIY operation because in the public mind a TV ad that's naff suggests that the product is as well.

Targeting television

When you buy television time you have a choice of 13 target audiences, with categories like 16–34 year olds, housewives, housewives and children, or an upmarket group like ABC1 men. You also have a choice of dayparts, broken down into daytime, early peak, late peak and night-time. Naturally, peak times are most expensive, and there are also variations according to the time of year. The biggest demand is for the run-up to Christmas, so the price of airtime shoots up. You can also advertise in different geographical regions, with London being the most expensive. And, as with most marketing, to really have an impact your advert has to be seen a number of times, which means buying multiple slots.

Most small and medium-sized enterprises probably will do better to spend their marketing budget on the other media that we have already considered. However, if you do want to explore the possibility of using TV ads, you can approach production companies directly or go via an ad agency that will work closely with such a company. Either way, you will have final say on the script, casting, choice of director and so on – the client is always right, but is well advised to let the experts do what they do best.

Who will deliver your message?

In television, as well as in radio and print, the use of a spokesperson or even a fictional character can help make your adverts distinctive. The spokesperson can be the head of the company, an employee or a celebrity. As mentioned earlier, there are some risks involved. Some company executives have woken up one morning to find that their expensive celebrity has been arrested on drugs or drink-driving charges, hardly the sort of associations you want with your business. And if the company spokesperson becomes ill or dies suddenly, there is a gap in the business's image. That's one reason why many companies have relied on a fictional character, such as the persona 'Captain Birdseye' for the frozen foods brand or Churchill the bulldog for the insurance company of the same name.

Another factor is cost. The bigger the celebrity, the more expensive the endorsements and appearance fees. Mascots, on the other hand, never ask for a pay rise, no matter how famous they get.

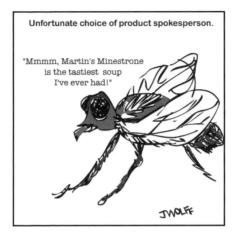

Unfortunate choice of product spokesperson.

"Mmmm, Martin's Minestrone is the tastiest soup I've ever had!"

JWOLFF

Direct response television

Direct response TV ads are designed to get the viewer to take some immediate action, either to phone or to go to a website for more information or to order the product. This can be in the form of a short advert or half-hour infomercials. The latter often include some kind of demonstration of the product, perhaps in front of an enthusiastic live audience. They generally feature a lively host, a fun atmosphere and frequent mentions of the freephone number that viewers should ring. The advantage of this kind of advert is that it's easy to test whether it's working. If the phones are ringing, it is; if they are not, it's not. While you may associate this format with juicers, vegetable choppers and weird exercise devices, more recently mainstream companies including Direct Line, Britvic and Fiat have been using direct response TV as well.

Along similar lines are the shopping channels that used to pop up after most people had gone to sleep. Now they are available around the clock on satellite and cable television. As well as the forced atmosphere of fun, they often feature a countdown for how many of the items are available, or for how many minutes you have left to phone in to order them. This 'ticking clock' deadline has proved to be a good motivator. It's also a great format for testing the appeal of products. Again, the ringing (or not) phones immediately give a measure of the popularity of the item being touted. These days the most popular shopping channels are selective as to which products they allow on the air, and they have been single-handedly responsible for the huge success of certain product lines, often those fronted by a celebrity popular with the older viewer.

Expert interview
George Lois on advertising and life

There are not too many heroes in the advertising world, but George Lois qualifies. His 'I Want My MTV!' campaign transformed the fortunes of the then struggling rock videos channel almost overnight. He's worked on huge accounts and tiny ones and I think his insights apply to every mode of traditional media. I had the pleasure of interviewing him some time ago in the offices of Lois/USA in New York City.

The notion of using a surprising or unexpected image is one of the themes running through much of your work. My first contact was the often shocking **Esquire** *covers you designed. For people who are not familiar with them, they included Andy Warhol drowning in a can of Campbell's soup, Lieutenant Calley, the US Army officer found guilty of ordering the My Lai Massacre in the Vietnam War, surrounded by Asian children and Mohammed Ali as St Sebastian. What was the philosophy of those covers? What was the big idea behind them?*
I thought of it as package design that stopped you dead in your tracks at the news-stand and raised hell.

One of the interesting things you say in your book, **The Big Idea,** *is that 'too many advertising professionals believe the visual image, the picture, is our common language. Not so. Our common language is always language.'*
You have to think with words. Even for the *Esquire* covers, I thought with words and then translated them into images. When you see Ali with arrows in him, you think of St Sebastian.

I look for three or four or five or six words that express the big idea, often combined with a strong image. Together, they create something that hits you hard, that you remember.

Advertising likes to think of itself as a wild and crazy creative business, but ironically often it is deeply conservative. How do you translate these ideas into advertising and how do you get away with it?
I'm able in advertising to do the kind of work I want because in many cases the people who come to me are in deep shit. They are the best clients because they say, 'Help!'

Years ago a terrific computer company called Data General was in trouble – great products but marketing problems. I did a pizza box campaign. Mainframe in a pizza box – we had guys going around with their product in a pizza box, and in the advertising world that had the same shock value as Lieutenant Calley did on the cover of *Esquire*. If you've only got $5 million and you're up against companies like IBM who are spending $100 million, what do you do? So I 'get away with it' because they really need to break through.

I'm interested in how you approach these challenges. What's your starting point?
I say to myself, here's a problem. I gotta come up with an idea that immediately impacts it, where overnight – in a day, in a week – people will think differently about it, and the press will pick up on it. If you have that in your head, when you get an idea like that, you get a surge. It means setting an ambitious goal for it. You have to perceive in your mind and in your eyes and your soul how things will be once this is seen. It's like an athlete seeing himself going over the pole. Most people don't see anything, they just start doing things. That can apply to anything, not just to an advertising idea. Look at it the way the rest of the world will look at it. That's different from the way a lot of people approach the process.

A long time ago there was a producer/director here named David Susskind. He had a very good show on Sunday where he talked to people, and he asked me to take part in a show on advertising. Two of the top advertising agency guys were there. One question was, 'What is advertising?' One of the guys went on for about five minutes about marketing and all that. The other guy also had a very nice answer and ended up by saying that advertising is saying, 'Buy me.' Susskind looked at me and said, 'George, how come you're making faces?' I said, 'I think these guys are in a different business.' He said, 'Well, what do you think advertising is?' I said 'I think advertising is poison gas. It should attack your nervous system – it should make you cry, it should rip out your eyeballs, it should rip out your lung, it should make you drop to your knees!' If you have that attitude about your work, then maybe you can do some things that change the world.

So that's what creativity is. Most people in communication don't understand that. It's very hard to teach creativity. So instead they teach advertising as a science. In fact it's an art. So the people coming into the advertising business, the magazine business, are all scientists because they've all done courses in communication and marketing. They think you can figure everything out, you can research everything, you can find out what people are thinking. Their minds are constipated.

Some people might say, well, this is all great if you have millions at your disposal, but you've done this on some pretty tiny budgets when you started out, haven't you?

One of the very first things I did with my own agency in 1960 – the silliest thing I've ever worked on in my life. The company was pickled green beans, called Dilly Beans. They had something like $5,000. I did things like 'Break the Smoking Habit', and showed a woman smoking a bean. I had a commercial that said if your local store doesn't carry Dilly Beans, knock something off the shelf. We were getting calls from retailers all over the city saying, 'Take that commercial off, people are knocking things off the shelves.' There was an article in *Time* magazine using this as an example of the power of advertising. Suddenly these things started selling and the woman who owned the company sold it to General Foods for something like $6 million.

That's hilarious. Can you give us another example where the idea was bigger than the budget?

I did a campaign in New York in 1966 for stockbrokers Edwards and Hanley. They went from almost no recognition to number one. We did a three-week campaign. I did one in which one kid says, 'My Daddy's an astronaut,' and another kid says, 'My Daddy's a fireman.' The third kid says, 'My Dad works for Edwards and Hanley.' The other two look at him and say, 'Wow!'

Finally, I have to ask you how you have managed to be on the top of your business for so long. Marketing and business require a lot of energy – what's the secret of not burning out?

I burn out every day! I go home physically exhausted – if I'm not, I haven't done my job. You're supposed to burn out. Then you replenish yourself and you go back the next day. I don't want to overdo the work ethic, but it's incredibly important. If you don't feel that way, you're not doing your job.

Marketing for Entrepreneurs

Marketing power boost

Check your image

Gather together all of the print-based marketing materials and forms you use. This includes anything that has your business's name on it: business cards, invoices, envelopes, packing material, signs (take photos if the signs are fixed to something or are too big to bring in), banners, brochures, etc. Look at them as a whole. Are they consistent in colour, typeface, style – or are you using a mixture of some old designs and some newer ones? Even if they are consistent, do they create the image you want?

Be brave and take the most typical piece and show it to half a dozen people who know nothing about your business. You can accost them on the street, if necessary. Offer them a small reward, like a £5 coupon to use at the nearest Starbucks or Pret A Manger, in exchange for a few minutes of their time. Ask them what three words first come to mind when they see your promotional material – what impression do they get from it? Write down every answer, whether you like it or not. If you have too much trouble remaining neutral, ask someone else to do this and bring you the list. Are these the terms you'd hoped to hear? If not, what do you need to do to create the image you'd like? If you don't know, hire a good graphic designer for a couple of hours to go through your materials and give you tips. If you're uncertain about where to find a good designer, look around for logos and business identities that you find effective and ask who created them.

If you feel the designer's input is on the right track, hire them to re-design all your materials and in the future stick to the template the designer will create. When you have a consistent and strong brand design, people will gradually become familiar with it – and familiarity is a step in the direction of trust.

Key points

→ Traditional (offline) media may not be glamorous but are still effective.

→ Your paper image is important and must be consistent.

→ Promotional strategies include giveaways, surprise discounts, coupons and hiring stands at trade fairs.

→ Targeted print ads and direct mail campaigns are powerful and easy to test.

→ Radio is an underestimated medium.

→ TV ads are expensive but excellent, especially when you want a wide reach.

Next steps

What action will you take to apply the information in this chapter? By when will you do it?

_____

_____

_____

_____

You're wasting half your marketing money – but which half?

Chapter Nine

There's an old saying, 'I'm wasting half my advertising money – the problem is, I don't know which half.' The same applies to marketing. If you're doing all manner of marketing activities it's very difficult to know which ones are working, unless you measure. It has always been possible to test and now the internet makes it even easier. With facts and figures coming back to you almost instantly, it becomes possible to continuously modify and improve your techniques.

What to test

What do you need to test? The answer to the question is, everything.

If you have a blog, you can see where your visitors are coming from and maximise your use of the most popular sources.

If you have a shop, you can test its physical layout, the effects of signage and various product price points.

If you send out an email message, you can send it to half your list with one subject line and to the other half with a different subject line and see which one is opened by more people.

If you put several videos up on YouTube, you can see which ones get the most traffic and put up more with the same topic.

If you use pay-per-click ads on search engines like Google, Yahoo! or MSN, you can try out various keywords and short phrases that go with the keywords. You'll see which ones people click on the most and, importantly, which ones result in the most sales or other action you want visitors to your site to take.

When selling online, you can easily try out different price points, different product combinations and the effects of various bonuses.

Most important of all, testing can help you to decide how to allocate your marketing budget. Here's a crucial thought expressed by Jeff Hayzlett, vice president of Eastman Kodak: 'It's not about the cost per page; it's not about the cost per e-mail; it's not about the cost per phone call; it's about a cost per response.' In other words, results are what matters and what should guide your spending, and results are measurable.

Let's take a closer look at a few of the most productive methods of testing.

Split testing

As mentioned above, it's easy to try out various versions of a website or online sales pages using split testing, in which some of the visitors see one version and some see another. This is called an A/B split test. For instance, if you are selling a beauty cream, headline A might be, 'What would it feel like to look ten years younger instantly?' and headline B might be, 'Would you like to know the beauty secret of Hollywood's top stars?'

The most important statistic you're looking for is the conversion rate – that is, the percentage of the people who click on your site who go on to take the action you want them to take. This might be buying a product or simply giving you their email address and name so that you can market to them afterwards. If you get 100 visitors to your site and 10 of them take the action you want, your conversion rate is 10 per cent. If you make a change and the conversion rate goes up, you will want to keep that change but also test it against new alternatives. For each test, the winner becomes the new standard, also called the 'control'.

You can do the equivalent offline, too, of course. If a certain advertisement that includes a coupon results in an average of 100 sales, which you will know because people will have to hand in the coupon at the time of sale, that is a standard to measure against. Next time you can try an advert with everything the same except for the headlines, and see whether that results in more or fewer customers coming in. You also should track how much each of those customers spends. It may be that headline A brought in 100 customers and headline B brought in only 50. On the face of it, headline A is the clear winner. But if the 100 people attracted by headline A spent, on average, £10 (for a total of £1,000) and the 50 attracted by headline B spent, on average, £30 (for a total of £1,500), then the latter is doing a better job.

Monica's husband is concerned she may be considering using split testing inappropriately.

Keeping track of variables

Of course, there are lots of variables. For example, if you tested two adverts designed to bring people into your shop and one ran during a week when the sun shone every day and the other during a week when it was pouring down with rain the whole time, the weather may have been a much greater factor than your headlines. The fact that the real world includes so many variables over which we have little or no control makes testing more complicated.

In other words

A **variable** is any element of a website, sales letter, advert or other marketing message than can be changed in order to determine what effect it has, if any, on how people respond. Variables include wording, colours, placement, prices and timing.

Online, it's much easier to control most of the variables. For instance, one company tested whether it was more effective to offer customers who came to its website a percentage discount (15 per cent off total purchase) or a coupon for a set amount (£25 off total purchase). The company knew that based on its customer's average orders, these would be roughly equivalent. It did a mailing in which half the list was offered the flat amount off, while the other half was offered the percentage discount. Everything else in the two messages was the same and they went out at exactly the same time. The result: the £25 off coupon had a 72 per cent higher conversion rate and generated 170 per cent more revenue. Why? Possibly because a flat amount is instantly understandable, whereas one has to calculate whether a 15 per cent reduction is worthwhile. Whatever the reason, it was a generous return for a simple test.

A little difference can make a big difference

You may be surprised at how much of a difference even a small element can make. As reported in *Online Strategies* magazine, one business was selling a collaboration software product from its website and decided to test the wording on the order button: 'Sign up now'; 'Start Now'; 'Organise me'; and 'Start Sharing'. The last one was a late addition that nobody expected to do well. However, it was the clear favourite and had a bigger effect on conversion than any other factor. In the case of West Coast Golf, the company that used the haggle button (see page 156), it tested the best wording to put on the button. 'Make an Offer' worked better than 'Buy for Less'. The company tested the best colour for the button. Blue got more clicks than red or green. It also tested the position. Right above the add-to-cart button was most effective.

Google to the rescue

A terrific free tool for this type of online testing is the Google Website Optimiser. It allows you to test several different elements at once. You can create a number of web pages with different combinations of headlines, photographs, prices, background colours and so on. You need to have quite a few people going to your site in order to find the strongest combination – the more variables, the more visitors you need. This is called multi-variate testing and it can get rather complicated. Certainly at first, it makes sense to focus your testing on one or two elements. Google has complete instructions for using the tool on its site and it's not as daunting as it may seem.

Jot down the ways in which you might use split testing in your business:

_____

_____

Surveys: what to ask, what not to ask

Your customers can be a great source of information and ideas. Surveys are one way of questioning them.

You can use formal or informal surveys to find out what people like and dislike about your product or service and what they think of your customer service. You can do this in your retail space, out on the street, via your website or emails, or in your blog, vlog or podcast. If you have their addresses you can do it via printed surveys. If you have their phone numbers you can do it via telephone. To increase the response rate, either give a valuable report or other incentive to all respondents or award a larger prize to a randomly selected one.

In the *Harvard Business Review*, Alex Lee, president of OXO International. wrote: 'We have done simple surveys in the lobby of our building by offering free OXO products in exchange for people's opinions. If Procter and Gamble's researchers saw us doing that, they'd say we were crazy for interviewing unscreened New Yorkers in an unscientific sampling. But we uncover great insights – in fact, we find that our small samples often echo the voice of the market.'

One thing *not* to ask is, 'What new product do you want or need?' Most people simply are not good at imagining something that doesn't exist yet. Did people know they wanted an iPod before it existed? Would they have said it would be great to have a touch screen that allows you to move pictures with a brush of your finger? Would games players have described wanting what turned out to be the Wii? Probably not.

In an interview with *Strategy + Business*, Booz & Company partner Alexander Kandybin put it this way: 'Understanding consumer needs is important in developing many products, but it's a difficult way to come

up with truly breakthrough ideas. Dependence on understanding consumers' own perceptions of their needs for innovation ideas will only
lead to incremental innovation, and incremental innovations can't, by
definition, reap large rewards.'

However, people generally *are* adept at describing their problems.
By paying attention to those issues, you will be able to come up with
ideas for profitable products and services.

As mentioned in Chapter Two, Survey Monkey (**www.surveymonkey.com**)
offers a free online survey service with which you can ask up to ten questions per survey and get up to 100 responses. It also offers a
professional version for about £10 a month, for which you can create a
survey of any length and get back up to 1,000 responses. Whether or not
you sign up, you can get a free 106-page user manual that will give you
an excellent grounding in survey design, as well as various ways of collecting responses and analysing data.

Danger!

In your surveys, avoid biased wording or questions that
include an assumption. For instance, 'What do you most
dislike about public transport in your area?' will elicit only
negatives, while 'What's your opinion of public transport
in your area?' will produce a more balanced response.

Next: prototype and test

Once you have extrapolated what people already enjoy and what might
solve their problems or respond to their aspirations, you can create a
prototype and test their response to that. Most people find it much easier
to discuss something specific and tangible than to respond to a mere
description. For example, a publisher was in conflict with an author about
what kind of cover would appeal to potential buyers. The publisher got
an artist to mock up three possible covers. Because the book's target
market was museum-goers, the publisher arranged to leave all three
covers in a museum shop along with a brief questionnaire asking people

which version they would be most likely to buy. There was a clear winner that went on to become the actual cover. This is a good example of how you don't necessarily need a formal, expensive focus group to get quick, practical feedback.

By testing reactions, refining and testing again, you can let the customer lead you to a successful innovation.

Spread the word

The results of a survey can sometimes make a good hook for a press release, but only if there is at least the semblance of impartiality. A press release revealing that in a survey of 200 randomly selected people, 25 per cent would rather eat biscuits than have sex might get a mention on a slow news day, but the result that 25 per cent would rather eat your brand of biscuit than have sex would be suspect.

What do you want to know?

What three key questions about your business would you like to have answered from the perspective of customers or potential customers?

_____

_____

_____

What type of survey could get you this information?

_____

_____

Observing

One of the simplest methods of gathering information is simply watching people's behaviour. What they do is a far better indicator than what they say. If you have a retail outlet, where do your customers go first?

What items do they pick up? Which ones do they put down again quickly? How much time do they spend in the different parts of the shop? What questions do they ask the salespeople?

When you're running a business it seems there's seldom time to just observe, but it's worth making the time or getting someone else to do it. OXO International president Alex Lee noted: 'At OXO, we've found that the user research doesn't need to be rocket science. What's important is that managers be inquisitive, that they be avid users of the types of products we sell, and that every employee be looking out, constantly, for problems and solutions in both the company's and competitors' products.'

As I grow older, I pay less attention to what men say. I just watch what they do. ANDREW CARNEGIE

If you have been observing the behaviour of young people for a few years, you will have noticed how much they enjoy keeping in constant touch with their friends, especially through texting on their mobiles. In response to this, in 2006 someone came up with Twitter, a free social networking and micro-blogging service that allows users to send and read other users' brief messages (up to 140 characters in length – characters, not words). These messages can be delivered via instant messaging, email, Facebook and others. Many people use it just to keep their friends informed of their activities hour to hour, but it's also being used by the BBC and CNN to disseminate breaking news, by a variety of businesses to let customers know of sales and by political parties for messages to the party faithful. It has even spawned a new type of anxiety, 'Twitter Stress', because, as the *Wall Street Journal* noted, 'Some users are starting to feel too connected, as they grapple with check-in messages at odd hours, higher cell phone bills and the need to tell acquaintances to stop announcing what they're having for dinner.' Nonetheless, it's clearly something many people want. As of the end of 2008, more than 5 million accounts had been registered. If you want to see whether any of these people are discussing your business, you can use **www.Search.Twitter.com**. You can also search for keywords that relate to your business to find out what people are saying about those on Twitter.

People who use **Twitter** call their short messages 'tweets.'

You probably think you don't have time, but setting aside one afternoon a month just to watch people can pay big dividends. Go where your customers go, eavesdrop, notice what interests them and what they enjoy. Take a notepad and jot down anything that occurs to you, but don't force it. Often inspiration strikes when we're just sitting and watching the world go by.

What could you observe that might guide you towards fresh ideas about marketing your business more effectively?

Marketing power boost

Ask key questions

Ask everyone who has anything to do with your business to jot down three questions for which they would like answers. Don't let them censor themselves because they don't know how you'd find out these answers; just ask them what knowledge would allow them to do their job better, to improve your product or service or to increase profits. Collect all the answers. Eliminate duplicates or very similar questions and cluster questions according to their topic. Then brainstorm which of the methods in this chapter would work best to yield the answers. It may require a combination of, for example, a survey in-store, split testing on your website and observing consumer behaviour in the real world.

Start the ball rolling. What three questions would you like answered?

_____

_____

_____

Key points

→ It's vital to test every aspect of your marketing.

→ Split testing allows you to measure the impact when you change an element of your message.

→ Google Website Optimiser allows you to compare multiple variables.

→ Surveys are an excellent tool for gathering information about your customers and their problems.

→ Observing how your customers behave can be more productive than simply asking them questions.

Next steps

What action will you take to apply the information in this chapter? By when will you do it?

_____

_____

_____

_____

Networking made easy (or at least easier)

Chapter Ten

What do you think of when you hear the word 'networking'? For a lot of us it brings to mind a group of vampires getting together over drinks, each trying to be the first to suck the other's blood. It doesn't have to be that way!

The key fact that makes networking so important is simple: people like to work with and buy from people they know. Therefore, you have to make yourself known to people who might be in the market for your product or service.

The networking secret

If you are networking-phobic, I can tell you the one secret that will not only make you a terrific networker, but will also allow you to enjoy it:

→ When you meet people, forget about what they can do for you and work out what you can do for them.

I don't mean what you can do for them if they hire you or buy your product; I mean what you can do for them with no strings attached.

If you have this in mind, you will lose all self-consciousness as you meet new people. Ask them about themselves and their business. As you listen, try to work out how you can help them in some way. This might mean you'll send them an article you've read recently that might be interesting and relevant to them. Or you might tell them about a product or service, not your own, that has impressed you and might be good for them. If nothing else, you should send them a note the next day saying you enjoyed speaking with them.

Of course, you'll probably also tell them what you do, but it won't be a hard sell, just a point of information. By all means, swap business cards, but remember that you want to know how to contact them for one reason: so you can do something for them.

This approach is counter-intuitive, but just give it a try the next time you go to a meeting or conference. Ninety-nine per cent of the other people there will be busy trying to push themselves. You will be an oasis of calm, the one person who actually listens to what the other person says instead of waiting for them to stop talking so you can do your pitch. You can also show interest in topics other than business. If the person you're talking to mentions their hobby or favourite holiday spot, chat about that.

All this is a lot easier when attending an event where networking is not the only function or even the main function. When something else is going on, such as a charity event, you immediately have a topic of conversation with strangers and there is not the mad pressure that sometimes characterises networking evenings.

Networking is not one of Victor's strengths.

How a therapist applied the secret

The approach I'm suggesting was inspired by a wonderful story about the late Milton Erickson. He was a fantastic therapist who created his own sometimes eccentric methods. They worked. A lot of what developed into Neuro Linguistic Programming (NLP) is based on Erickson's work.

On one occasion he was counselling a young woman who had just started attending college. She didn't know anybody there, she was painfully shy and she was depressed. He gave her a prescription not for a drug but for a task. She had to give three other students a compliment every day. It could be about anything: something someone was wearing, or something they had said, or their prowess at a sport or how well they told jokes. But it had to be genuine, not empty flattery. She followed the prescription. Three months later she was one of the most popular people on campus.

It's no wonder this worked. How often do people really look at us and listen to us, not to catch us out or to wait until we've finished so they can resume talking, but to notice something they like about us? And how often do they pay us a genuine compliment? In my experience it's pretty rare. I'm suggesting you follow in the footsteps of this young lady. When you next go to a networking event, a meeting or a conference, do the same thing. Give at least three genuine compliments. By the end of the evening you will probably be one of the most popular people there. And, as we know, people buy from people they like.

> ## The currency of real networking is not greed but generosity. KEITH FERRAZZI

Networking strategies

Here are a few additional networking strategies:

→ Don't stay at the bar while consuming your drink.

→ Hang around near the food. Most people attending a meeting will go there sooner or later, and as a small-talk opening you can make a comment about the refreshments.

→ When you already know some of the people at a meeting, introduce them to each other. They, in turn, will be more likely to introduce you to people they know but you don't.

→ When people ask you what you do, tell them not only what you do, but also why you love doing it and how it relates to your larger goal or mission.

→ Use a business card that is distinctive and will help people remember you. At the end of an evening they may have collected a few dozen cards and the next day will have forgotten who was who. If yours stands out they'll be more likely to remember you. One of my cards reads, 'That tall writer you met...', with my name and all the contact information below.

→ Jot down a memory-jogger on the back of any card you collect as soon as you've finished talking to that person.

If you're not great at small talk, conversations can easily falter after 'And what do you do?' Go prepared with a few open-ended questions in mind, such as 'What's the part of your work you enjoy most?' or 'What's been your greatest success?' or 'What's your ultimate goal for your business?'

Danger

Expert interview
Rosina Ledger Berman on natural networking

For an additional perspective on networking, I turned to an old friend, Rosina Ledger Berman, principal of public relations agency RSB International. She has worked in both the United States and the United Kingdom and has been my PR representative and informal networking coach.

Rose, let's start with the obvious question: how important is networking, especially networking in person?
It's been true since the beginning of any kinds of societies – we like to deal with people we know, like and trust. I don't see any reason for that to change. And even if we soon will be communicating on little wrist-video screens, there will never be a substitute for looking someone in the eye and getting a sense of who they are. So, yes, it's extremely important.

You're a naturally gregarious person, but there are some people who are shy and find networking in a group difficult. Do you have any advice for them?
It's a skill that can be learned even if you feel awkward about it at first. Toastmaster's Clubs have helped many people become confident public speakers even if they had a fear of public speaking. That's an organisation I always recommend. The dues are minimal and the members are friendly and welcoming. I believe sometimes they assign you a mentor if you want one, who will give you one-to-one advice and feedback. If you need more help there are acting coaches, personal coaches and therapists who can all be useful.

Another thing I recommend is that people invest in at least one really smart outfit. That applies to men as well as women. It may sound shallow, but it's a fact that wearing something that makes you look good also makes you feel good. It's a confidence-booster. These things help not only with networking but with making presentations to clients or your colleagues or the media, all of which may be required of entrepreneurs at various points.

One of the issues is small talk, knowing how to start a conversation. Any advice on that?
You know, I think it's the same as with dating situations. People think you have to be clever or say something unusual or witty, yet often the thing that works the best is just a simple, 'Hello, my name is,' or a comment about the food, or even that favourite British standby, the weather. It's just a way to get a conversation started. If you're nervous, admit it – say something like, 'I'm really nervous at these kinds of events, but I promised myself I'd talk to at least one person, and I guess it's you.' That will usually get a chuckle and you may find the other person feels the same. By the way, one other strategy is to go with a friend or colleague who is more outgoing and let him or her start the conversations. You can agree beforehand that once you're talking to someone, your colleague will wander away.

I want to ask about one other aspect of introductions – what's come to be known as the 'elevator speech'. Lots of people suggest that you prepare some kind of pithy statement about what it is you do.
Certainly that's useful, but in my opinion there has been a bit too much emphasis on making such a statement dramatic in some way. Instead of saying 'I am an accountant', you're supposed to say, 'I help people realise their financial dreams.' Personally, those kinds of statements make me feel a bit queasy. Yes, to say simply, 'I am an accountant' is boring and doesn't give the other person a lot of impetus to say anything other than, 'Oh'. So you might say, 'I'm an accountant and I specialise in helping people find legal ways to pay less tax.' That probably will prompt them to ask whether you've found any good ways to pay less tax and then the conversation has started. When I tell people I am in public relations and I represent primarily entertainers they always ask, 'Anybody I might know?' So the idea is to give people enough information to lead to a logical question.

Of course, don't get so carried away telling your story that you forget to be interested in them as well. It's a cliché but true that the topic people find of greatest interest is themselves. If you allow people to talk about themselves they will consider you a fascinating conversationalist.

If someone says they just can't be bothered with going through all that – perhaps they're happy being introverts and don't really want to change – what options do they have?

I'd suggest two. One is to focus on one-to-one meetings. Many people who are shy in groups are fine with that. Identify someone you want to get to know and simply invite them to lunch. If you're too shy to ring them, send them a letter. Make it clear that this is not a sales call – you just admire something they have done or the way they run their business and would like to have a chat. Then follow through with that. Have some questions in mind about their background, how they've achieved whatever they've done and so forth. They will ask you about yourself and your business, but don't give them a sales pitch. Just get to know them, and at the end pay the bill, thank them, and follow up with a note offering to be of help to them any way you can.

The other option is simply not to network. Life is too short to spend it doing things you hate. Delegate it. Find someone in your company who is outgoing and send them out there to represent you. If you're very shy, make it a part of your personal brand to be a bit mysterious. The reclusive genius is an interesting character for most people.

Online networking

These days a lot of people do their networking online. The biggest social sites are Facebook and MySpace, but it's LinkedIn that is expressly for business users. In mid-2008 it had 25 million users and was continuing to grow quickly. Its average user is older and wealthier than the typical Facebook and MySpace user, and you won't find pictures of puppies and lists of favourite tunes on members' profiles. The point of LinkedIn is to exchange information, ideas and opportunities. On its website, it explains its service in this way:

> When you join, you create a profile that summarises your professional accomplishments. Your profile helps you find and be found by former colleagues, clients, and partners. You can add more connections by inviting trusted contacts to join LinkedIn and connect to you. Your network consists of your connections, your connections'

connections, and the people they know, linking you to thousands of qualified professionals. Through your network you can:

→ *Find potential clients, service providers, subject experts, and partners who come recommended;*

→ *Be found for business opportunities;*

→ *Search for great jobs;*

→ *Discover inside connections that can help you land jobs and close deals;*

→ *Post and distribute job listings;*

→ *Find high-quality passive candidates;*

→ *Get introduced to other professionals through the people you know.*

The basic service is free, although it does offer paid accounts with more functions. Based on my own experience, the main problem is that you will be approached by a lot of people you don't know who want to join your network. If you admit them, the idea that every member can vouch for the people on their network goes out the window. However, it can still be an extremely useful way to make connections and find and be found, so it's definitely worth putting up a profile.

How groups can help

There are also groups on LinkedIn based on similar business interests and associations. My tip is to join not only the groups who are doing what you do, but also more importantly, the groups comprised of people who might need your product or service. Don't start marketing to them brazenly, but do pay attention to what's bothering them, what trends are taking place and any other information that might help you in your other marketing efforts. You can also use the site's 'ask and answer questions' feature to pose questions – another great opportunity to do research about your niche. By answering questions within your expertise, you establish yourself as an expert and make it more likely that when they need what you're offering they'll come to you instead of to someone else.

There are other business-related networks, including Xing, which is more European-oriented, and Ecademy, which has strong representation in the United Kingdom, especially among consultants and small business owners. The UK-based Talkbiznow adds productivity tools to the mix. It's best, at least at first, to start with one of the well-established sites and expand from there.

On all social websites, if you just get on there to shamelessly advertise your business, you'll turn people off. If you make it your mission online to do the same thing I recommended for offline networking – that is, to be of service – rich rewards will come in time.

Don't forget the gatekeepers

Strictly speaking, dealing with gatekeepers isn't networking as such, but it's important. Gatekeepers are the people who control access to decision makers. Their title may be receptionist, personal assistant, secretary or something else, but what they have in common is that they wield a lot of influence. It may be hidden but it's real. Also, they tend to be overworked, underappreciated and underpaid. If you treat them well you will stand out. You might be amazed at how many people treat them brusquely, even rudely, just because their job titles are modest. But if you treat them badly and then ring them up to request access to their boss, guess what happens? The boss is in a meeting, or they're too busy, or they'll have to ring you back. Sometime.

It was years ago while working as an intern for a major airline that I saw first hand how many subtle ways gatekeepers have of advancing or hindering the progress of the people who have to go through them. Naturally, you should treat such people with respect anyway, but as well as being the decent thing to do, it can pay dividends. Here are some ways you can win over the gatekeepers without overstepping the mark:

→ Respect their time. If they sound hassled and you have a long message to leave, ask whether they'd like you to call back or to call you back.

→ Learn and use their names.

→ Don't take your frustration out on them. If their boss is not giving you what you want, it's not their fault – at least not if you've been nice to them.

→ If they are especially helpful, give them a small token of thanks. When I worked in film and television in Hollywood, the tradition was that you sent a basket of fruit, wine and cheese to the bigwigs you were dealing with. These extremely well-paid people needed a basket of food like they needed a hole in the head. Instead I sent the baskets to the secretaries I dealt with throughout the year. They were delighted and always mentioned to their bosses what a nice person I was to deal with. Hmm, do you think that might have helped position me in the minds of their bosses as well? Naturally, any gifts should be modest, otherwise it will look too much like a bribe.

→ Keep track of where they go. In some businesses, it's not unusual for today's PA to be tomorrow's vice president, or at least PA to someone else with whom you might want to do business. If you know they are leaving their current job, find out where they're going and send them a note of congratulations on their new position.

The bottom line: gatekeepers, as well as anybody with whom you network, generally will treat you the same way you treat them. Be nice, be helpful and it will bring benefits.

Marketing power boost

Take charge of networking

If you don't like attending other people's networking events, why not set up one of your own? You can choose the venue and time that work best for you and make it by invitation only. Leave out lots of promotional literature for your own business, but focus on creating a fun, welcoming and interesting event rather than just a pitch-fest. One idea: invite a guest speaker who will provide value for everybody who attends and allow time for an hour of mingling and conversation afterwards. The speaker's presentation will provide an easy conversation starter for everyone concerned. I've spoken at several such events and have always found the atmosphere to be much more relaxed than at the speed-dating kind of networking meetings.

Key points

→ The secret of effective networking is to focus on how you can help others.

→ Online networking saves time and gives you global reach.

→ Joining online groups related to your business allows you to find customers and business partners, and to get help with your marketing challenges.

→ Don't forget to cultivate the gatekeepers who control access to people you need to reach.

Next steps

What action will you take to apply the information in this chapter? By when will you do it?

_____

_____

_____

_____

The power of outsourcing

Chapter Eleven

Having read about all the effort that goes into marketing, you may be wondering how you can possibly do it all. The answer is, you can't. Not by yourself, anyway, if you still want to have time to cover all your other responsibilities. That's where outsourcing comes in. While it may sound like just another word for 'getting someone else to do it', what's new these days is that that someone may be halfway around the world. There are skilled people in India, Eastern Europe and Africa, as well as in the UK, the United States and just about every other country in the world, who offer their services via the internet. There are also companies that ensure that such transactions are safe both for the person hiring and the one being hired.

Why outsource?

One of the reasons why it makes good sense to outsource is that it will help you take advantage of the Pareto principle, which you read about in Chapter Two. As you will recall, the Pareto principle says that 80 per cent of your value comes from 20 per cent of what you do. If you put more of your time and energy into doing that 20 per cent, you'll have to get someone else to take on the tasks you are shedding. One best-selling book, *The Four-Hour Work Week*, suggests that you can outsource so many things that you have to work only half a day a week yourself. This is unrealistic for most of us, but the principle is valid. Ricky Thomas, founder of PedMeds, which sells medical supplies online for pets, told the *Sunday Times*: 'Getting the right people with the right skills in to free up your time is so important. The temptation to do everything yourself is strong but it's a false economy.' He reported that the company's accountant paid for himself very quickly in terms of finding grants and the work he has done with suppliers. Thomas also used the web to find affiliates – that is, people who sell his products for a commission.

What can be outsourced?

Just about any aspect of marketing and administration can be outsourced, including:

→ accounting services;

→ handling routine questions via phone or email;

→ designing logos and other graphic projects;

→ designing websites;

→ search engine optimisation (making your website more popular with search engines);

→ writing copy;

→ producing audio or video;

→ conducting surveys;

→ doing split testing;

→ writing press releases;

→ publicity and promotion.

Which of the above tasks do you think you might want to outsource?

_____

_____

_____

To outsource effectively, you must find the people who have the necessary skills and are willing to do the work for an acceptable price. You must also communicate your needs clearly, monitor their progress and give them feedback so that you get exactly what you want.

> ## I hire people brighter than me and then I get out of their way. LEE IACCOCA

Finding the right people

Undoubtedly you're already familiar with the traditional methods of finding freelancers to do work for you. These include going through job agencies, approaching universities, asking colleagues to refer you to reliable and skilled people and placing advertisements in trade or general circulation publications. In this chapter we'll focus more on using online sources.

Online services: Elance

One of the longest established and most reliable online services is elance.com. On its website you'll see the tremendous range of skills and services offered in these major categories: web and programming; design and multimedia; administrative support; sales and marketing; finance and management; legal; and engineering and manufacturing. In just the web and programming section it has almost 30,000 people registered to do that kind of work. At the time of writing, it had had more than 20,000 new projects posted in the last 30 days.

There is no charge to buyers for using the service – Elance collects its fee from the service provider when you pay for the work. If you're new to Elance, it does take a $10 deposit, which is automatically refunded after ten days. Once you've registered, you can post an assignment in any of the categories. As an example, let's say you want to get someone to design a logo for you. You give a good description of what you want – for instance, colour or black and white, a style if you have one in mind and an idea of how and where it will be used, as well as how long the winner will have to complete the work.

You also give a maximum price you are willing to pay. If you're not sure what budget to use, you can browse what other buyers on the site have paid for similar work. In order to win the assignment, bidders can bid lower than that figure. For instance, let's say you indicate you are willing to pay $500 for a logo (the fees are calculated in US dollars). You may get several bids for that amount, but you might also get one for $375, another for $350 and another for $200. Most bidders will provide links to their portfolios so that you can assess the quality of their work. You will also be able to see how many other projects they have completed via Elance and how those buyers rated the work. Typically you'll get lower bids from new providers because they are less of a known quantity.

You will get more bids if you use Elance Escrow, a free service designed to protect both the buyer and the provider. The buyer's funds are held securely until the services are provided satisfactorily by the provider. The provider can begin working on a project knowing that the fee is in the escrow account.

Elance allows buyers and bidders to communicate via the site. When you have enough bids you can decide to whom to award the contract, you can cancel it if you feel nobody came up with a good enough bid or you can extend the amount of time for bidding.

Once you accept a bid the work can proceed. If you are happy with the work and want to use that provider again, the next time you have a project you can invite them specifically to bid on it. There are also procedures in place for the buyer or the provider to use if there is any dispute about whether the work was done in accordance with the agreement.

Example: writing a report

To give you an example of how it works in practice, I wanted someone with knowledge of the legal field to write a report for me on how to protect written material, such as manuscripts and screenplays. I posted a description on Elance, including what the report should cover and that it should be approximately 5,000 words long. I also specified that all rights to the material were to be signed over to me, which is important if you hire someone to write or design something, otherwise that might become a point of contention. I received half a dozen bids. The one I chose was not the cheapest, but it was someone who had legal training and had written other articles on similar topics that I was able to read in his portfolio. I put the fee of $175 (approximately £120) into escrow and released the money when the report was sent to me and I'd found it satisfactory.

Other online services

I've gone into some detail about Elance because most of the services have similar procedures. Here are some others to consider:

→ **RentACoder.com**. As the name suggests, this site, founded in 2002, specialises in people who can develop custom software. It has more than 200,000 providers on its books and has essentially the same procedures and safeguards as Elance. I used RentACoder to find someone to help develop a website. This was not quite as satisfactory as my Elance experience, but the fault lies with me. Although I found someone who was able to do everything I specified, he was not very good at suggesting the best way to do things. I was not clear enough in my initial description. I should have indicated that I'm not very technical and wanted someone who could advise on the construction of the site, not just carry out the technical aspects. This underlines the importance of being absolutely clear and complete in your description of what you want.

→ **Guru.com**. Providing services similar to Elance, this service has more than 1 million registered members and more than 100,000 active freelancer profiles. It has some interesting additional features such as online video profiles for providers.

Before you place too much trust in a provider you may want to try a little test. Select one relatively small task that is typical of what you want to outsource. If you want someone to write a long report, start by commissioning a short one. Give the same assignment to the three providers who you think are the best. Yes, you'll pay for the same job three times over, but you also will have had direct experience with three people or companies and will be able to decide which one will make the best member of your virtual team.

Using interns

Even though outsourcing via the internet is the more revolutionary development, there is still a place for more traditional approaches. One good option is using interns.

Unfortunately, the use of interns has sometimes had a bad reputation because some employers consider them to be handy, free labour to exploit for mundane tasks like photocopying and making tea. However, when it's set up properly, an internship can be extremely useful to both sides. You get:

→ an enthusiastic, eager to learn helper;

→ a fresh viewpoint on your business;

→ a potential employee later on.

In return, the intern should expect to get:

→ a mentoring relationship;

→ exposure to real-world business;

→ a good reference;

→ potential employment prospects later on.

For these to result, you need to be clear from the start how you would use the services of the intern. Although their tasks can include things like doing the photocopying and running errands, there should also be the opportunity for them to learn skills and participate in, or at least observe, the meaningful aspects of how your business is run. If you set out clearly during the interview what is involved in the internship, it will give you and the prospective intern a chance to see whether you are in accord. If you establish a set of goals and deadlines right at the beginning, it will be easier for you to monitor the intern's work and give useful feedback, and easier for the intern to be sure that your needs will be compatible with the demands of their studies.

The hours and any remuneration should also be specified at the start. Some internships pay expenses only, including transportation, meals during working hours and any equipment or wardrobe needs. Other internships pay an hourly salary or bonuses upon the completion of specific projects.

Some universities, colleges and academies have a structure in place for placing interns. At others you can approach the professors or lecturers in the most relevant subject areas and let them know you are looking for an intern. You can also post notices on campus bulletin boards or student sites online. For marketing-related tasks you might be especially interested in students studying business, advertising, graphic design, computer science (especially website design) and journalism. It's likely they'll be familiar with the internet and using social sites like Facebook, so getting them to help you build an online presence is one obvious possibility.

When doing interviews have at least one other employee or colleague in the meeting, ideally of the opposite gender to you. It's rare, but sadly once in a while there are misunderstandings or false accusations of inappropriate behaviour in such situations. Having a witness present should prevent that from happening. You will also need to find out whether having an intern on your business premises requires any additional insurance coverage.

Using retired or semi-retired workers

Another traditional approach to consider is hiring retired or semi-retired people. These days people who have retired are not so keen just to sit back and watch television or play golf, and in many cases they need some kind of income to augment their pensions. They represent a great resource for the entrepreneur because they bring a wealth of real-world experience to the job. The same general guidelines that applied to interns apply here, although in this case you would definitely expect to pay them an hourly wage.

To find such workers you can post notices at community centres, put adverts in your local newspapers and ask your current employees whether they can recommend anyone. You can also check with local public relations and advertising agencies whether they have any employees who have recently retired or are working part-time and might be interested in freelancing for you.

Danger!

Our natural tendency is to hire people who are like ourselves. However, you're hiring someone to do the things you don't do well, which may well call for not only a different set of skills, but also a different personality from yours. Make sure the person you hire matches the tasks, not you.

Why people don't outsource

The biggest objection most people have to outsourcing is a belief that, 'It'll take me less time to do it myself than to teach someone how to do it.' That's true – the first time or two that the task is done. But in the long run you will save an enormous amount of time. Allocate the time to give guidance and feedback and very shortly the benefits will begin to flow.

The other obstacle for some entrepreneurs is the fear that the person to whom a task is delegated won't do it the same way they do. Again, that's quite possibly true. But what's your priority – getting it done the way you would do it or getting it done well? As long as the outcome is acceptable and the method has no negative effects, what difference does it make? Focus on the outcome and let people get there in the way they prefer – they may do it even better than you!

Time saver

When you are training someone to take over a task you are doing yourself, make a written record of the process as well. If you ever need to replace that person, this document will short-cut the process.

Your turn

Which three tasks or functions are you most likely to want to outsource? For each one, also indicate where you think you are most likely to find the desired help (online, student intern, retired worker).

_____

_____

_____

Marketing power boost

Outsourcing what you hate to do

There is a close correlation between what we like to do and what we do
well. This means that if you can outsource the things you hate to do, they
will probably be done better than you would do them. For the next week
keep a notepad handy and each day jot down what you are
procrastinating about or doing but not enjoying. At the end of the week
you will have a list of things to outsource. Pick out the one you'd most
like to get rid of and find someone else who can do it. Monitor their
efforts until they are handling the task well. Then go on to the next item
on the list. If you encourage your employees or colleagues to do the
same, the results can be outstanding because everyone will be focusing
on their strengths and finding others to do what they don't do so well.

Web bonus

At our website, **www.forentrepreneursbooks.com**, click
on the 'Marketing for Entrepreneurs' button. On the link
for Chapter Eleven you'll find an audio track with more
tips for outsourcing effectively.

Key points

→ You can't do it all yourself. Focus on doing only what you do best.

→ Online outsourcing gives you access to expertise around the world
and allows suppliers to bid on the work you need.

→ Interns are inexpensive and can bring fresh thinking to
your business.

→ Retired or semi-retired people can bring extensive experience to
your business.

Next steps

What action will you take to apply the information in this chapter? By when will you do it?

_____

_____

_____

_____

Putting it all together

Part Three

Create your one-year marketing master plan in 60 minutes

In this chapter, you can put together all the information you've already come up with in the rest of the book. Rather than just copying what you've written down already, refine your answers – based on having read the entire book and thinking about all the facets of marketing. By collecting this information in one location you will be creating the raw material for your one-year marketing master plan. As you bring your plan to fruition you can return to your answers for guidance and inspiration.

We will go through it step by step, and in Chapter Thirteen you will decide how you will divide these major steps into six-month, three-month, one-month and weekly marketing goals to suit your situation. Of course, many of them are not one-time tasks but will continue to be a part of your ongoing marketing campaign.

Cultivating a marketing mindset

The Goal: To instil a marketing mindset in everyone in your business.

The Benefits: Marketing becomes an integral part of the business, not something limited to one department. You get a steady stream of fresh marketing ideas. A consistent focus on benefits increases customer satisfaction.

The Method: Once a month, review your efforts to make sure that they reflect the following principles:

→ Your marketing messages focus on the *benefits* of your product or service.

→ You get 80 per cent of your results from only 20 per cent of your efforts – so it's important to know what that 20 per cent is for you.

→ The best time to conduct a marketing campaign is – always. Marketing has to be a continuous and consistent part of your business.

→ Great ideas can come from anyone, so be open and listen before making marketing decisions.

→ The way to make an impression in today's crowded marketplace is to do something different – as long as it's congruent with your product or service.

→ The only way to know what's working is to test and never stop testing.

→ When some aspect of your marketing isn't going well, work out why and apply that learning.

→ When some aspect of your marketing is working particularly well, work out why and apply that to whatever you do next.

→ Don't give up easily on your goals but do be flexible about how to achieve them.

→ Be honest with yourself about what aspects of marketing you want to handle, and would handle well, and outsource the rest – but use what you've learned in this book to monitor what others are doing for you.

Determining your USP

The Goal: To determine or create a unique selling proposition that distinguishes your product or service from that of your competitors.

The Benefit: Customers understand the rationale for buying your product or service over all others.

The Methods: Analysis of unique aspects of your product or service; if necessary, brainstorming further differentiation. Creating clear USP statement to guide development of all marketing materials.

Draw on your notes from Chapter Three to answer these questions:

1 What is the single most attractive or appealing thing about your product or service?

_____

2 What is the single biggest benefit to the user of your product or service?

_____

3 What is your best statement of your USP?

_____

If you haven't already done so, get your existing customers as well as some potential customers to respond to this USP. Do they find it accurate and compelling? If not, revise it.

Identifying your target audience and finding them

The Goal: To identify the niche(s) to target.

The Benefits: Marketing is focused and cost effective.

The Methods: Analysis of possible target markets using key criteria. Analysis of best ways to reach them.

Draw on your notes from Chapter Four to answer the following questions:

4 Who most needs your product or service?

_____

5 Who will be most receptive?

_____

6 Who can afford this product or service or is authorised to buy it?

_____

7 With whom do you (or the company) already have credibility?

_____

8 What is your best brief description of the target market that you will focus on?

_____

9 Which three or more print magazines are these people most likely to read?

_____

_____

_____

10 What are three or more online sites they are likely to visit regularly?

_____

_____

_____

11 What are three or more types of place they are likely to spend some of their leisure time?

_____

_____

_____

12 When they have a problem, what are three or more sources of information they are likely to use?

_____

_____

_____

PR, publicity and word of mouth

The Goal: To identify and employ the most effective strategies and methods of getting free publicity via public relations, publicity and word of mouth.

The Benefits: Maximum credibility, low cost compared to advertising and high visibility.

The Methods: Creating powerful press releases, targeting key publications and other media, appearing on radio and TV as an expert. Cultivating influencers and giving them incentives to spread the word. Creating appropriate publicity events.

Draw on your notes from Chapter Five to answer the following questions:

13 Who will be handling press releases and other public relations duties for your company?

_____

14 If you will be outsourcing this, who will you ask for referrals to effective PR freelancers or companies? (Who have you noticed getting good press attention?)

_____

_____

_____

15 Which one newsworthy event or topic could you promote with a press release in the next 30 days? Describe it using the key points described in the relevant section of Chapter Five, including a catchy headline. (Note: you will be aiming to generate at least one press release per month.)

_____

_____

_____

16 Which publications and sections within those publications are most likely to be interested in this press release?

_____

_____

_____

17 Which radio or TV stations and shows on those stations are most likely to be open to having you, or someone else from your business, as a guest? (Note: you will be aiming to set up one such appearance per month.)

_____

_____

_____

18 What incentive will you give for people to contact you (e.g. a useful report)?

_____

_____

_____

19 Who are the influencers in your field who could be most effective in spreading positive word of mouth about your business? (You can list them by name or by general description – for example, if you own a night club, taxi drivers might be good influencers.)

_____

_____

_____

_____

_____

_____

20 What incentives will you give these influencers to spread your message?

_____

_____

_____

21 What ideas do you have for a publicity stunt or event that could promote your business? (Note: you will be aiming to create one such event at least every three months.)

_____

_____

_____

Telling your story

The Goal: To tell the story of your product or service and what it can do for customers in a powerful manner.

The Benefit: Customers will have an emotional involvement with the product or service and be more loyal.

The Methods: Employing the key motivators to develop customer loyalty. Tapping into an existing story or creating a new one using the Hollywood 'hero's journey' model.

Draw on your notes from Chapter Six to answer these questions:

22 What is the main emotional appeal of your product or service?

_____

23 What useful thing could you give prospective customers to trigger the reciprocation effect?

_____

24 What could you get prospective customers to commit to that might lead to a later sale?

_____

25 Where can you get named testimonials from customers or clients that will act as social proof?

_____

26 What elements of your business will help customers to see the similarity between you and them – to take advantage of the likeability/similarity effect?

_____

27 Who are the authorities your customers respect?

_____

28 How might you get those authorities to endorse your business?

_____

29 How might you be able to use the scarcity effect genuinely?

_____

_____

_____

30 Is there an already existing story that your product or service fits in with? If so, summarise it here:

_____

_____

_____

31 Do you plan to be part of the story by being a spokesperson for the business? If so, how?

_____

_____

_____

32 Use the hero's journey structure to tell the story of someone who solves a problem or takes advantage of an opportunity by buying your product or service. To construct the spine of that tale, answer the following questions:

→ Who is the hero of this story (male or female – a typical customer)?

_____

→ What is the problem or opportunity and what makes them aware of it?

_____

_____

→ What is the first step the hero would take?

_____

→ What kind of allies, helpers or mentors would the hero encounter? (This could be your product or service.)

_____

→ What kind of obstacles and enemies would the hero overcome with the help of your business?

_____

→ What would be the moment of truth, when the hero realises all the promised benefits of your product or service and finally overcomes the problem?

_____

→ How will things be better for the hero upon their return to the normal world?

_____

33 Jot down three hopes your product or service might tap into:

_____

_____

_____

34 Jot down three fears your product or service might help assuage:

_____

_____

_____

35 How would you describe the problem that your product or service solves? (Hint: what is it like? What's a good metaphor?)

_____

_____

36 How would you describe your solution? (Again, can you come up with a metaphor that evokes an image?)

_____

_____

37 What's the best thing about your product or service?

_____

_____

Using the new media

The Goal: To employ new media to gain customer awareness, brand familiarity, trust and new paths to sales.

The Benefits: Market penetration at relatively low cost, ability to reach specific niches and sub-niches with accuracy and ability to personalise marketing messages.

The Methods: Using e-bulletins, blogs, vlogs, podcasts and website, together with presence on social media sites as appropriate, in a mix with traditional media.

Draw on your notes from Chapter Seven to answer these questions:

38 What kind of information or entertainment that is relevant to your business would your customers value?

_____

_____

_____

39 What kind of personality would be most appropriate for an e-bulletin for your business? (Examples: authoritative, informal, gossipy, humorous.)

_____

40 How often would you be prepared to send out an e-bulletin? (Choose between weekly, every two weeks or monthly.)

_____

41 Who in your business would be most qualified and capable of writing your e-bulletin? Or would you outsource it?

_____

42 For the kind of information or entertainment that is relevant to your business and that your customers would value, which format do you think would be most appropriate – blog, vlog, podcast or viral video? (Of course, you can choose more than one.)

_____

43 How often would you be prepared to post on your blog or vlog and/or produce a podcast?

_____

44 Who is the person in your business most qualified and capable of doing this? Or would you outsource it?

_____

45 Other than networking, what are two or three ways that you might benefit from using sites like MySpace and Facebook?

_____

_____

_____

46 What are three things you could do to improve the content of your website?

_____

_____

_____

47 What are your plans for doing a search engine optimisation (SEO) check on your website?

_____

_____

_____

48 What are half a dozen keywords and phrases that might be most relevant to your product or service?

_____

_____

_____

49 How could you use your website, social media or other new media approaches to improve your customer relations?

_____

_____

_____

Traditional media

The Goals: To employ traditional media to gain customer awareness, brand familiarity, trust and new paths to sales. Establish consistent image across media.

The Benefits: Ability to reach larger audiences, capitalise on perceived glamour of radio and television and achieve clarity in minds of customers regarding your product or service.

The Method: Development of a strong paper image, using print ads, coupon marketing, trade shows, direct mail, radio and television, as appropriate, in a mix with new media.

Draw on your notes from Chapter Eight to answer the following questions:

50 Are you happy with your paper image (logo, letterhead, etc.)? If not, what do you need to do to change it?

_____

_____

_____

51 What role, if any, do have in mind for print ads?

_____

_____

52 What role, if any, do you have in mind for coupon marketing?

_____

_____

53 At which trade shows, if any, do you plan to exhibit?

_____

_____

_____

54 If you're planning to exhibit at trade shows, how will you make your stand more interesting so it attracts visitors?

_____

_____

_____

55 What role, if any, do you have in mind for direct mail?

_____

_____

56 What role, if any, do you have in mind for radio ads?

_____

_____

57 What role, if any, do you have in mind for television?

_____

_____

Testing

The Goal: To continually maximise the effectiveness of all marketing materials to get best results at lowest cost.

The Benefits: Continual improvement in effectiveness of marketing materials and better awareness of needs and desires of target population.

The Methods: Using split testing, surveys and observation.

Draw on your notes from Chapter Nine to answer these questions:

58 How do you plan to employ split testing in your business?

_____

_____

_____

59 What are three key questions about your business that you would like to have answered from the perspective of customers or potential customers?

_____

_____

_____

60 What type of survey could get you this information?

_____

_____

_____

61 What could you observe that might guide you towards fresh ideas about marketing your business more effectively?

_____

_____

_____

Networking

The Goal: To increase awareness of the brand and its benefits among the target population through networking.

The Benefits: Greater awareness, more referrals, a larger circle of contacts to call upon for help or advice and a potential stock of future customers.

The Methods: Attending networking events and using online networking sites such as LinkedIn.

Draw on your notes from Chapter Ten to answer these questions:

62 Which networking events do you plan to attend?

_____

_____

_____

63 Which online sites (such as LinkedIn) do you plan to use for networking via the internet?

_____

_____

_____

Outsourcing

The Goal: For every employee in the company to be able to focus on their strengths.

The Benefits: Outsourced tasks done more cheaply and more time for top 20 per cent of tasks that can bring exponential growth.

The Methods: Using online services such as Elance and RentACoder. Hiring students and retired or semi-retired workers to do tasks that are not the best use of your time or that of your current staff.

Draw on your notes from Chapter Eleven to answer the following question:

64 Which three tasks or functions are you most likely to want to outsource? For each one, also indicate where you think you are most likely to find the desired help (online, student intern, retired worker).

_____

_____

_____

In the final chapter you will see how you translate the marketing master plan into tasks to do daily, weekly, monthly and twice-yearly.

Now just do it!

Chapter Thirteen

Do you want to know how to be more effective than 95 per cent of the people who pick up a marketing book? Here's the answer: actually *do* the work in this chapter. Most people will think that creating and carrying out a marketing plan is a great idea – and then they won't make the time to do it. A 2002 survey by Royal Bank of Scotland found that 12 per cent of small business owners in Britain worked more than 70 hours a week. The more challenging economic conditions since then mean that the situation has, if anything, become worse. By now *you* know that marketing is part of the solution, not part of the problem. By targeting your audience effectively and by using all of the media at your disposal to give them a compelling reason to do business with you, you will bring in more revenue even in these tougher times. When you take action, you go right to the head of the pack.

Now let's put it all together. First things first. Marketing is a means to an end – it's time to get specific about what you really want from it.

1 What specific outcomes do you want your marketing to achieve for you in the next 12 months? (State this in any measure that is significant for you. It can be a money amount, a percentage increase or anything else that you equate with success.)

_____

_____

_____

2 With that in mind, what specific outcome would you like to have reached in six months? (It may be exactly half of what you want for the one-year period or, if it might take some time to gain momentum, it might be less. Again, express this in whatever measure is meaningful to you.)

_____

_____

_____

3 Same question – this time for three months from now.

_____

_____

_____

4 What about one month from now?

_____

_____

_____

5 What part of that would you like to achieve in the next seven days?

_____

_____

_____

6 Finally, what part of this week's goal can you achieve over the course of today or tomorrow?

_____

_____

_____

The next question concerns what marketing methods are most likely to get you to your goal. Every person reading this book will have a different goal, so I can't prescribe an exact programme for you. However, if you have done all the exercises, you will have a pretty good idea of which of the many techniques covered is the best fit for you and your goal. And what I can do is lay out my suggestions for three levels of marketing activity that you can adapt to your needs.

Level one is the minimum you should do if you're serious about marketing your business, and it's geared to the one-man band. If you are a freelancer or a one-person business, it's unrealistic to expect that suddenly you'll find 20 hours a week to spend on marketing. Level one assumes that you'll be able to spend about half a day a week.

Level two is the middle-of-the road option – realistic for a small business in which the marketing tasks can be split between two or three people, to add up to the equivalent of one person working one full day per week. This should get you good results within your niche.

Level three is the luxury model. It assumes that, however you split it up, the equivalent of one person's eight to ten hours a week will be dedicated to marketing, but with outside help so that your role will be more supervisory. With that kind of commitment, you will get serious marketing oomph.

Again, all of these are just rough guidelines. I encourage you to mix and match to come up with the formulation that best fits you.

The essentials

Before we even get to level one, you must:

→ cultivate the marketing mindset;

→ determine your USP;

→ identify your target audience and where to find them.

If you haven't done these three tasks, you have no solid basis for a marketing campaign. Even if you have loads of money to invest, there's no point in putting up a fancy website if you don't know who you hope to attract to it. There's no point in spending money on telling people about your product if you haven't decided what makes it different from what everybody else is offering. It sounds like common sense, but you'd be surprised at how often people rush out and get beautiful, expensive letterhead and brochures printed before they've thought through what they're trying to achieve or who will be looking at those glossy flyers.

Level one: not much time, not much money

→ Get a solid website. It doesn't have to be all-singing, all-dancing – in fact, it shouldn't be. But it should give people a good idea of who you are, what you do and why it's so great. They must be able to reach you through it and to find their way around it easily.

→ Put your story on your website. I'm talking about a story that gets across your USP with emotion and flair, maybe a story that makes a hero out of customer. If you're not much of a writer, visit a writers' group and listen to them read their work. When you find someone whose words are full of the right kind of fire, ask them for help. If money is tight, do a barter deal or at least buy them a pizza. Most writers will be thrilled to have someone who admires their words, and when the money starts rolling in you can pay them a bonus.

→ Monitor the publications that cover your segment or business. Note the names of the journalists who write for them regularly. At least once a month, send them an email complimenting them on one of their articles or making an interesting comment.

→ Write at least one press release every quarter, geared to publications that your target group reads. It needs a hook but should also tell, or at least allude to, your USP story. Send it to the same journalists that you've been cultivating over the months.

→ Make at least two radio appearances or speeches to groups per year to spread the story while you are entertaining and/or informing them.

→ Create a blog on which you post twice a week in an entertaining and/or informative manner. It can be one of the free ones, technically simple, but it must have bags of personality, otherwise it won't get any attention. Guess what needs to come through? Yes, the story.

→ Get at least one endorsement or testimonial per month from a satisfied customer or client. If someone says something good about your business, ask them to put it in writing and then ask permission to quote them. Don't worry, asking gets less embarrassing the more often you do it. Put these testimonials on your website and on your blog's 'about' page.

→ Write at least one article a month for ezinearticles.com or a similar site. Again, if you need help, find a writer. Be sure that your bio box links to both your site and your blog.

→ Do an annual check-up of your paper image. Find a graphic design student whose portfolio you like and ask them to upgrade your paper image if it needs it.

→ Attend at least one trade show or professional conference per year. You don't have to take a stand – just go and soak up everything

Now just do it!

that's happening and that you can steal, er, adapt. Which stands have the action? Why? Which stands are Sunday morning dead? Why? What giveaways are people flocking to grab? When you're ready to host a stand yourself, you'll have had a great education in what works and what doesn't. If the conference is expensive and you're short of money, see whether your local newspaper will give you a press pass in exchange for an article or two about the event.

→ Test at least one aspect of your marketing every month. It can be an offer via your website or something in your shop, if you have one. Whatever it is, there will be one thing that you are continually trying to improve.

→ Go to at least one networking event per month with the attitude and homework assignment I suggested in Chapter Ten (see page 212). If there isn't one in your area, start one.

→ Find at least one new thing every month that you don't do well or hate to do and outsource it. An intern may be just the right answer.

→ Every three months, sit down and evaluate which of the above methods has yielded the most dividends. Do more of that one.

Level two: a bit more money, a bit more time

Implement all of the above, with the following changes or additions:

→ Add material to your website at least twice a month, even if only your online articles.

→ Write six press releases a year.

→ Do four radio appearances or talks to groups per year.

→ Have at least a blog, but if it suits your business, consider a vlog and put the best of your videos on YouTube as well – search engines love video. If you don't have a vlog, make at least four videos a year for YouTube and the other sites served by TubeMogul. Also host them or at least link to them on your site.

→ Get at least one audio or video testimonial per month. If you get the testimonial over the phone, you can record it easily using Skype. Put these on your website and blog.

→ If it's appropriate to your business, exhibit at one trade show or conference a year. Try to get a speaker's spot as well – often that's included in the deal.

→ Have at least three elements of your marketing under constant testing.

→ Go to at least two networking events a month. Alternatively, go to one and then once a month invite one person you'd like to meet to lunch.

Level three: luxury edition

Implement all of the above, with the following changes or additions:

→ Get a search engine optimisation expert to review your site and tweak it as necessary twice a year or more.

→ Retain a public relations consultant to write your press releases and distribute them at the rate of one a month.

→ Come up with at least one publicity stunt a year that will get your company talked about – in a good way.

→ Host at least one charity event per year in the name of your company. Rotate the charities, so that you'll meet a greater variety of patrons and sponsors.

→ Ask your PR person to try to arrange a regular guest spot for you on a local radio station, or to place a monthly column that you will write or someone else will write under your name.

→ Retain a webmaster who can keep several elements of your site or AdWords pay-per-click campaign under constant review and testing. They can also be adding fresh content to your website and your blog several times a week.

→ Record half a dozen videos a year for the video sharing sites, with content that will be of interest to your target group. Then get a DVD made of a collection of these videos and use it as a promotional item.

Now just do it!

At all three levels I'm talking about the quantity of your effort, but what really matters the most is the quality of your efforts. It's better to send out one great press release a year than six boring ones. So, when I suggest that you write four press releases or make six videos, naturally I mean four fantastic press releases and six superb videos.

One more time: the importance of action

I hope you've enjoyed reading this book – and have highlighted lots of things and become excited about the marketing ideas I've shared with you. But if you now put down the book and don't do anything concrete, it will have been mostly wasted time.

I strongly suggest that you get a big calendar and use it as your planning and execution tool. Go back to the big goal you expressed at the start of this chapter. Break it down into 12 chunks and write those down, one for each of the months of the year.

Then take each of those monthly goals and break them into four or five chunks and note them on the weeks of each month.

Finally, break those weekly goals down into daily tasks. For each chunk, decide which of the marketing tools discussed would be the most likely to give you the results you want.

For instance, let's say you sell burglar alarms. A good goal would be for you to become recognised as an expert in this field. One tool that would help you achieve that would be giving talks on safety, initially to anybody who will listen. It would also make a terrific topic for an outspoken blog or podcast. If you can make some videos demonstrating ten tips for burglar-proofing your home, and do it with a bit of humour, that might well turn into a hit on YouTube. It would also be worthwhile trying to get bookings on local radio, as crime is always a popular topic on phone-in shows.

The next step

Whatever your goal, there are marketing tools that can help you reach it. In this book I've mentioned the importance of having a story. Mine is that I get great satisfaction from writing books and giving work-shops that help other people realise their dreams. I hope in some small way this book will do that for you and will continue to be a kind of coach by your side as you go forward. If you'd like to stay in touch, please contact me at **jurgenwolff@gmail.com**. I look forward to hearing about your success!

Index